THE BLUE WILLOW INN COOKBOOK:

EXPERIENCING THE SOUTH

by

LOUIS AND BILLIE VAN DYKE

A COLLECTION OF RECIPES FROM THE RESTAURANT
VOTED BEST SMALL TOWN RESTAURANT IN THE SOUTH BY
THE READERS OF *SOUTHERN LIVING* MAGAZINE

1

THE BLUE WILLOW INN COOKBOOK:
EXPERIENCING THE SOUTH

By Louis Van Dyke and Billie Van Dyke

Printed in the United States of America
First Printing November 1996
Second Printing January 1997
Third Printing May 1997
ISBN 0-9647867-8-8

Cover design: Glenn Ozburn of THP Printing and RA. Pacheco of Streamlight
Photograph credits: Photograph on page 11 courtesy of the Historical Society of Social Circle, Georgia; Photographs on pages 42, 43, 133, 173 & 181 of the cookbook text and pages 5-7 of the photo gallery courtesy of Darrell L. Huckaby; Photograph on page 4 courtesy of King Features Syndicate. All other photographs are from the Van Dyke collection.

Published by
ST. SIMONS PRESS, INC.
P. O. Box 467603
Atlanta, Georgia 31146

DEDICATION

This book is dedicated to my foster mother, Annie Laurie Exley, who made me a part of her family and taught me the joys of helping and serving, and how to make every day special.

Billie Van Dyke

FRIED GREEN TOMATO HUNT ENDS
AT BLUE WILLOW INN
by Lewis Grizzard

A lot of people who saw the movie "Fried Green Tomatoes" probably asked themselves, "What's a fried green tomato?"

There wasn't any dialogue that I recall concerning fried green tomatoes in the movie--just a sign outside the Whistle Stop Cafe that advertised they were on sale inside.

The type food the movie dealt with mostly was barbecue, and if I go any further, I'd be giving away some of the plot for those who still haven't seen this year's "must see" movie.

Truthfully, I hadn't thought about fried green tomatoes in a long time until I saw the movie.

My grandmother used to serve them when I was growing up, but after I left home, I don't recall eating another one.

So I set out a month or so ago trying to find some place that still served fried green tomatoes so I could reacquaint myself with their taste.

I was in a restaurant in Jackson, Miss., that served fried dill pickles slices. For the record, they're a perfect munchy with a cold long neck bottle of beer.

Fried eggplant is easily located in the South. Fried okra, of course, is served in just about every place that features the meat.

But fried green tomatoes? I searched and searched. Nothing.

But then I had business this week in the hamlet of Social Circle, 35 miles east of Atlanta, off I-20. When lunchtime came I asked a local, "Where's the best place in town to eat lunch?"

"Try the Blue Willow Inn," I was told.

The Blue Willow Inn, on the main drag in Social Circle (do

4

they still say "main drag"?) was inside an old plantation-style home that obviously had been renovated recently.

The deal was $6.50 for all you could eat of any and everything sitting out on a couple of large tables.

I started with the sweet potato soufflé. I went to the baby lima beans from there. Then to the squash casserole, the green beans, the rice, and on to the turnip greens. My plate runneth over and I wasn't to the meats and breads yet.

I piled three pieces of fried chicken on top of that and added a piece of hot, buttered cornbread. Next to the cornbread was something I didn't recognize right away.

"This wouldn't be...?" I said to a waitress.

"Yessir," she replied. "They're fried green tomatoes."

I wound up eating 10 slices. The sweet sourness of the green tomato, quite different from the taste of red tomatoes, with the crust on the outside, was incredibly pleasing.

I talked to the proprietor, Louis Van Dyke, who said he had been in the restaurant business nearly all his life. He said he opened the Blue Willow last Thanksgiving Day.

I asked him about the fried green tomatoes.

"I was serving them a long time before the movie came out," he said.

He even brought me out a green tomato and told me he bought it in a farmer's market. You slice 'em, batter 'em, and throw 'em in the grease. Sounds easy in case somebody wants to try it.

I am a connoisseur of authentic Southern cooking, which is getting more and more difficult to locate. Half the time you think you've stumbled upon it, they serve mashed potatoes that come out of a box.

But not at the Blue Willow Inn in Social Circle.

If I gave ratings for Southern cooking, I'd have to give the Blue Willow my absolute highest mark--5 bowls of turnip greens.

Every dish was authentic and delicious, including the banana pudding I had for dessert.

I shall return.

Reprinted with special permission of King Features Syndicate

ISAIAH 44:8-9

Fear ye not, neither be afraid: have not I told thee from that time, and have declared it; ye are even my witnesses. Is there a God beside me? Yea, there is no God; I know not any.

They that make a graven image are all of them vanity: and their delectable things shall not profit; and they are their own witnesses; they see not, nor know; that they may be ashamed.

TABLE OF CONTENTS

INTRODUCTION
BY LUDLOW PORCH

Magicians are some of my favorite people. I have loved them all my life from Harry Houdini to Mandrake. I guess I like them so much because they can make wonderful things happen and you're never sure how they do it . . . it's magic.

My two favorite magicians are Louis and Billie Van Dyke. No, they don't make things disappear and they don't pull rabbits out of a hat, but every day they do magic things at The Blue Willow Inn.

They can wave their magic wand over a green tomato and turn it into a Southern delicacy that will make a possum smile. They know more about Southern Fried Chicken than Einstein knew about long division. No vegetable on the planet is safe from their wonderful magic.

Handle this book with tender loving care. It holds the secrets of the Van Dyke magic.

THE FOUNDING OF SOCIAL CIRCLE

(REPRINTED WITH PERMISSION FROM THE *LOGANVILLE NEWS JOURNAL*, AUGUST 17, 1995)

By Terry Prater, Staff Writer

When Mr. Joel Strickland of Tattnall County learned that he had drawn Lot Number 96, First Land District of Walton County, in the 1820 Lottery, he and his wife Elizabeth talked it over and decided not to keep the property.

Mr. Strickland was soon offered $118 for the 250 acres, and just five days after Christmas, Joel and Elizabeth signed the warranty deed making three men owners of the tract in southern Walton on which the town of Social Circle was to evolve. The second of these co-owners ran into debt, and in 1824, his one-third interest was bought at sheriff's sale by John P. Blackmon, one of the other original purchasers, for $11 or approximately thirteen cents an acre. Blackmon was able to buy the remaining one-third share, giving him sole ownership.

John Blackmon bought and sold several tracts in the new county, but he was especially pleased with Lot 96. On this property was an excellent spring, near which the important north-south rogue road was intersected by the best known route from the southwestern part of the county, Hightower Trail. Near the latter's ford on the Alcovy was the recently vacated campsite of a band of Creek Indians, whose choice of the location in itself spoke well for the region's fertility and comfort.

Blackmon added his own dwelling to those standing near the crossroads and donated a nearby parcel as site for a Methodist Church. Soon a small storehouse, the meeting house, and a shop gave the little settlement 10 miles south of the county seat the semblance of a village. It was a likely spot for business, for at the junction of the two old routes travelers often paused to rest. Friends frequently met, either by design or accident, and newly formed acquaintances were often renewed by the patterns of their travel habits.

Legend says that the settlement received its name when a new traveler, impressed by the exhuberant hospitality of a little group of congenial pioneers, remarked enthusiastically, "This sure is a social circle!" This may be true, however, a less colorful explanation should not be ignored. Another community by the name of Social Circle was brought to this section by a former citizen of the older village.

Early in January 1826, Blackmon and Augustine B. Pope "stuck" a chestnut stake in the ground and measured off an acre to include the shop already standing. Pope paid Blackmon $100 for the lot, and then Blackmon specified in the sale of the property that Pope "not carry on any business of a public nature only such pertains exclusively to an apothecary (drug) shop." The two men had discussed a site for a post office on the settlement and, on January 5, 1826, government authorization came through. John Blackmon was designated as Social Circle's first postmaster.

In 1832, Social Circle was incorporated. New settlers continued to move in and in June 1836, Mr. John Dally opened a grocery store in the city limits. During 1845, the Georgia Railroad reached this community as it advanced westward. The coming of the railroad was probably the most influential event in Social Circle's early history and marked this city as the county's first rail center. A Masonic lodge was established in 1848, and the first officer elected was the engineer who had surveyed for the Georgia Railroad.

In 1869, Social Circle was incorporated as a town and limits extended to one-half mile from the center of town in all directions. Town ordinances of 1869 required merchants to close at 10 P.M., and any person found on the streets thereafter must give a satisfactory account of himself or spend the night in the "guard house." Playing marbles on the Sabbath was prohibited, and sale of liquor on election days was illegal. Fines were given out for cock fighting, fastening horses to shade trees or fences, and for riding a horse in a "disorderly manner." The head of each household was required to keep a strong ladder long enough to reach the top of the highest building on his lot as a precautionary measure in case of fire, and dwellings on the public streets had to be underpinned so as to "keep out hogs and help abate the flea nuisance."

Main Street, Social Circle, Ga.

MAIN STREET, SOCIAL CIRCLE...THEN

Social Circle was highly publicized by a Supreme Court case shortly before the turn of the century, when the town became the center of a freight-rate controversy of national importance, where the railroads challenged a finding of the then-relatively new Interstate Commerce Commission. The court decision in this instance indirectly brought about another challenge of the Commission's powers, with the result that Social Circle's name was widely mentioned and repeated across the country for periods of years.

In 1904, Social Circle surrendered her 1869 charter and was subsequently incorporated as a city. Limits were one mile from the public well at the intersection of Madison, Monroe, Covington, and Gibbs Streets.

MAIN STREET, SOCIAL CIRCLE...NOW

Experiencing the Blue Willow Inn Restaurant and Historical Mansion

The Blue Willow Inn Restaurant is housed in a neoclassical Greek Revival mansion featuring a wide portico porch supported by four fluted columns with Corinthian capitals. Above the front door is a balcony supported by ornate brackets. The house was built in 1917 by John Phillips Upshaw, Jr., for his wife Bertha and daughter Nell. This was the second home built by Mr. Upshaw. His first home, on the same five-acre tract of land now housing the Blue Willow Inn, was a two-story Victorian cottage built in 1899. The five-acre tract had previously been the site of a tannery owned by his father, John Phillips Upshaw, Sr.

The construction of the mansion was prompted by the building of a Greek Revival mansion directly across the street from the Victorian cottage by John's younger brother, Sanders Upshaw, in 1916. Sanders in part owed his fortune to his brother John for loaning him money to purchase a cotton farm in the early 1900s. Not to be outdone by his younger brother, John and his wife Bertha measured Sanders's home inside and out during the final phase of construction and then drew plans to build their house a little grander than Sanders's house.

In order to do this, the Victorian cottage had to be moved. Trees were felled, and the cottage was rolled on logs to the lot south of John's five-acre tract. After moving the cottage, numerous wagon loads of dirt were brought in to raise the building site to the same height as Sanders's land. There was a natural slope, and by filling the site with dirt, the new home for John and Bertha would be directly across from Sanders's home and on the same level.

13

Several improvements were made in John's version of the house to better Sanders's house. For example, John's house was built with cream brick instead of wood; the roof on John's house was red tile, a roof that was superior to Sanders's slate roof. Sanders's house had only one side porch, while John's house had two. The double windows on Sanders's house were outdone by the triple windows with granite sills and beveled and leaded crystal glass fanlights on John's house. The oak floors in John's house were laid in a decorative pattern as opposed to Sanders's flooring which was laid in the typical side-by-side pattern. John Upshaw's house had to be just a little larger and a little better. In spite of the "one-upmanship" by John Upshaw over his younger brother, it is said that the families had a close and cordial relationship all of their lives.

A frequent visitor to the Upshaw's new home was Margaret Mitchell, author of *Gone with the Wind*. Ms. Mitchell stayed at the now relocated Victorian cottage while dating Redd Upshaw, her first husband. Redd Upshaw was a cousin of John Upshaw and lived nearby in Between, Georgia, and was supposedly the model for the character of Rhett Butler. The marriage of Redd and Margaret Upshaw was short, ill-fated and ended in divorce.

Picture of the Upshaw home as it appeared in 1920.

Having constructed what was generally considered the finest and best built house in the county, John and Bertha Upshaw lived there until their deaths. Mr. Upshaw made arrangements to bequeath the property to the clubs in Social Circle to be used as a community house after the death of his daughter, Nell. In 1952 Nell Upshaw Gannon deeded her life interest in the property to the clubs of Social Circle as she had no interest in maintaining the home.

From 1952 until the late 1960s, the house was the center of cultural, civic and social activities. Weddings, birthdays, school proms, graduation dances and most of the social activities in the community were held at the clubhouse. In the 1950s a baseball diamond was constructed in the back of the property.

During the late 1960s and early 1970s desegregation was taking place in the South, and Social Circle was no exception. Lawsuits were filed over the use of the community swimming pool, as it had been constructed with city tax money. During the turmoil of the era, the clubs abandoned the property and renounced title to the property. With the death of Nell Upshaw Gannon in 1974, ownership of the house and property went into the courts for clarification.

The Bertha Upshaw Clubhouse and Pool were abandoned and neglected from the late 1960s until 1985 when Reverend Harvey purchased it.

In 1985 the Georgia Supreme Court ruled that title to the property belonged to the heirs of the estate of Nell Upshaw Gannon. Reverend Homer Harvey, a Church of God minister, purchased the property from the heirs in 1985 and established the Social Circle Church of God in the mansion. In the late 1980s construction began on the rear of the five-acre tract to build a church, and in 1990 the Social Circle Church of God moved from the Greek Revival mansion to the church on the rear of the property. Reverend Harvey then deeded the church-occupied property to the church trustees and sold the main house and the balance of the property to Louis and Billie Van Dyke.

The fifteen years the property had been abandoned and tied up in the courts had taken its toll on the grand old mansion. Reverend Harvey had already spent large sums of money renovating the exterior of the house, replacing rotting wood and repairing the roof. Louis and Billie Van Dyke took up where Reverend Harvey left off. The house needed more roof repairs, extensive repairs to the columns and renovations inside. After repairing the main level, updating the wiring and plumbing and expanding the kitchen, the Van Dykes were ready to open their dream--the Blue Willow Inn Restaurant. The restaurant opened on Thanksgiving Day 1991.

During the next year, the second floor was renovated and transformed into dining rooms for banquets and group dining. In 1993 renovations began on the poolhouse and the pool, which had not been drained since the late 1960s. The poolhouse was expanded and converted into a gift shop to compliment the restaurant, while the pool was refurbished and accented with fountains. The pool and gift shop compound were then enclosed with wrought iron fencing.

The Blue Willow Inn Restaurant hosts some 4,500 to 5,000 customers weekly, serving a Southern buffet often proclaimed the best in the South. As guests enter the grand hall with the crystal chandeliers, they are escorted to one of the many dining rooms: the Savannah Room with its warm fireplace, the Garden Room which was formerly part of the back porch, the Sun Porch, the Charleston Room which is reminiscent of old Southern charm, the Lewis Grizzard Room which was named for the famous author and columnist who wrote about the Blue Willow Inn, and the Walton Room which is the largest room on the main level. The Walton Room is the buffet service area, and the Southern buffets served in the Walton Room are served in a catered style. Guests choose from an array of four to five meats, nine to ten vegetables prepared Southern style, soup, chicken and dumplings, salad fixings and homemade biscuits, muffins and cornbread. Last but not least is a delicious spread of pies, cobblers, puddings and cake.

The second floor houses the Magnolia Room, which is used for large functions and banquets. With seating for eighty, it is the largest dining room in the house. Two smaller rooms, the Blue Room and the Tea Room are also open to guests and small parties on the second floor.

The mansion is decorated in deep greens and burgundies which are complemented by antique furnishing and accessories. The walls are adorned with fine art and part of the Van Dyke's Blue Willow dish collection. The Van Dykes have been amateur collectors of the Blue Willow pattern china since the early 1970s, and their fondness of this pattern resulted in the name of the restaurant, the Blue Willow Inn. The tables are set with Blue Willow china and adorned with cut fresh flowers.

Guests at the Blue Willow Inn Restaurant are encouraged to absorb and enjoy the slower pace of the Old South. A visit to the Blue Willow Inn should be an experience in both dining and relaxing. From being greeted by Southern ladies attired in antebellum dress, to sipping lemonade while rocking on the front porch, guests are treated to genuine Southern hospitality of a bygone era.

Enjoy the gardens. Enjoy the Southern food. Enjoy the ambiance of the old Southern mansion. Relax for just a moment and let the world pass by. This is the Blue Willow Inn experience.

The former Bertha Upshaw Clubhouse, now gloriously restored and home of The Blue Willow Inn Restaurant.

"Seriously, if you think there's a chance you may not make it to heaven, then for goodness sake, try to make it to the Blue Willow Inn one time before you die."

Walter Albritton
Senior Pastor
Trinity United Methodist Church
Opelika, Alabama

"FEAR YE NOT, NEITHER BE AFRAID . . ."
The Story of Louis and Billie Van Dyke

From the time Billie was a small child, she had an interest in cooking and helping in the kitchen. Her mother, Nita Jane Baker, used to scoot her out of the kitchen and out of her way so she could prepare family meals, but when time allowed, Nita did teach Billie some of her cooking skills. Growing up on the banks of the Wilmington River in Savannah, Billie spent many hours with her father and brothers fishing, shrimping and digging oysters in Savannah's salt waters. When Billie was eleven years old, however, her father, Herman "Pop" Baker suddenly died of a heart attack; gone were the fishing days with her dad. Hard times set in for her family which now consisted of her mother, one sister and three brothers. Billie, the oldest child, had to help raise her younger siblings who ranged in age from six weeks to nine years old.

Serious illness beset her mother, and the family was scattered. Brothers Dennis and Jimmy were adopted and moved out of the Savannah area. Sister Dot was raised in a girls' home, and brother Charles was sent to Bethesda Orphanage in Savannah where he stayed until joining the Marines upon graduation from high school. Billie being the oldest, was "less adoptable" than her younger siblings. After going to the children's home for placement in a foster home, and in between, spending time with her mother whose health had improved, she spent the last years in high school with Marvin and Annie Laurie Exley in Garden City, a suburb of Savannah.

While living with the Exleys, Billie developed her cooking, entertaining and sewing skills. Mr. Exley taught Billie how to bake biscuits and cornbread and how to make them "look just like the pictures" on the packages of flour and cornmeal. Mrs.

Exley frequently clipped recipes from the newspaper and magazines and experimented with new dishes. Billie helped prepare
and cook the new recipes for visitors who frequently came to the
Exley's house and the minister and his family who usually ate
Sunday dinner with the Exleys.

During this time Billie met her first husband, William
"Bill" Edgerly, Jr. Bill was a student at Benedictine Military
Academy in Savannah. A courtship blossomed into marriage
when Billie was eighteen. From the time Billie and Bill were
first married, her home became the center of family activities
with her brother Charles, sister Dot, and their grandmother
"BaBa." Billie made friends with everyone she met, and she
found herself constantly entertaining friends and family. Cooking for large groups became a natural way of life for her.

In the first five years of her marriage to Bill, Billie's three
children were born: William III ("Chip"), then second son Dale,
and finally a daughter, Donna. Billie involved herself in church
work, school activities and the American Red Cross volunteer
swimming instruction program. The swimming instruction proved
to be the outlet Billie needed from homemaking while still including her children in her activities. Having received many
awards from the Red Cross for volunteer work, Billie took over
the swimming instruction and lifeguard program at the Port
Wentworth, Georgia, swimming pool. During this time she met
Louis Van Dyke, a volunteer swimming instructor. Louis became good friends with Billie's husband and was soon considered a friend of the family. No one would have ever dreamed
that a tragic event would eventually lead Billie and Louis to one
day marry each other.

In 1967 Billie's first husband suddenly died in a tragic
accident. Billie was now facing the same situation that her mother
had faced many years earlier. Left alone with three small children, she was determined to keep her family together. Times had
changed since her father had died—Social Security now provided

20

survivors' benefits. These benefits and a part-time job enabled Billie to continue to make a home for her children.

At the time of Bill Edgerly's death, Louis was entering active duty in the United States Navy. After being discharged from the Navy, Louis renewed his friendship with Billie and the children. From fixing screens to rehanging gutters and painting, Louis became the handyman around Billie's house; he also became a "big brother" to Chip, Dale, and Donna. After a couple of years the friendship between Billie and Louis grew into love, and Billie and Louis were married on May 1, 1970.

Just prior to the wedding, Billie's brother Dennis, who had been adopted 28 years earlier, appeared on Billie's doorstep with his wife and family. He was making the United States Army his career and had recently been transferred to Fort Stewart Army Base near Savannah. Dennis had remembered living on Wilmington Island as a small child and brought his family to Savannah to search for his family and his roots. Seeing a familiar house, Dennis discovered an aunt he did not know he had, Betty Cowart, and she directed him to his sister Dorothy Ann's (Dot) house in Garden City. After Dennis's reunion with Dorothy, she directed him to Billie's house. Soon thereafter, Billie was entertaining Dennis, his wife Liz and their children along with Billie's brother Charles, her sister Dot and their families. There was never a dull or boring time around the Van Dyke house; whenever there were social and family events, they took place at Louis and Billie's. Billie soon adjusted to married life and became a full-time mother and homemaker, happily entertaining family and friends.

In 1973 tragedy again struck Billie—her son Dale was accidentally shot and killed by his best friend. He was buried the day after what would have been his seventeenth birthday. Entertaining and thoughts of entertaining were over; a dark cloud settled over Billie, Louis and the children. In 1974, Louis left a business in which he had invested everything he and Billie owned, including mortgaging their home, and the business went bankrupt shortly thereafter. After the loss of Dale, as well as the loss of the business and their house, Louis and Billie packed everything they owned into the back of a rented moving van and moved the family to Atlanta.

Louis began a career in operations with a major Atlanta trucking firm, and both Louis and Billie became active in their church. Billie was again entertaining often, and in order to supplement the family income, she began a small catering business out of their home. Billie was soon doing weddings and parties, limiting herself to church friends and their referrals. In 1978, Louis and Billie were tiring of the typical suburban subdivision life of small lots and little privacy, and they began looking for several acres outside of Atlanta on which to build a house. In 1979 they purchased land in Walton County just outside of Social Circle, Georgia. Louis and Billie still joke that they had to move forty miles outside of Atlanta in order to afford a few acres of land. After finishing their home, Billie's part-time catering business became too busy to continue operating out of their home.

In the summer of 1985, Louis and Billie decided that it was time to move the catering business out of the house and into a catering facility. A small restaurant in an old house in Social Circle had already gone out of business. One of Billie's friends, Susan Pressley, knew that Billie was looking at the former restaurant and encouraged Billie to open a restaurant so the "girls" could get together for morning coffee. After looking at the house, both Louis and Billie agreed that it would make an ideal catering facility, and with some work it would probably make a good restaurant, too. A restaurant! Neither Louis nor Billie had ever given any thought to opening a restaurant, but after talking the idea over at length, they decided: *Yes, we can open a restaurant. Anybody can open a restaurant.*

The plan was that Louis and Billie would spend all of their spare time fixing up the house, redecorating its interior and cleaning the kitchen. Since Billie was a good cook and Louis was good at fixing things, they decided the plan would work. While Billie ran the restaurant and catering, Louis would continue to work at his job and spend his spare time helping run the restaurant. After all, someone had to wash the dishes and clean the floors.

Louis consulted with a good friend, Bill DeMoss, whose business skills he respected, and Bill was frank with Louis. "You do not have enough cash for a venture like this," he advised. He further cautioned that Louis was "undercapitalized and risked losing his savings." After having sought and considered the advice of someone he respected, Louis decided to open the restaurant anyway. After all *anyone can open a restaurant.*

After spending most of their savings and working three months to get the restaurant ready, Billie and Louis finally opened Billie's Classic Country Dining Thanksgiving week 1985. They both knew they *had* to make a go of it. Preparing the restaurant cost more than they had originally planned, and by opening day their savings account was down to a mere $800.00. The Van Dykes weren't worried, though, as they still had Louis's income from the trucking company.

Serving lunch and supper six days a week (the restaurant was closed on Mondays) began to take its toll on both of them. With only two employees, Billie was working sixteen hour days and between his job and the restaurant, Louis was getting only four to five hours a sleep nightly; however, they still needed Louis's paycheck. After the restaurant had been open for about three weeks, Louis fell asleep at the wheel driving home from work in Atlanta and almost hit a car head-on just a few miles from home; Louis was so exhausted that even the shock of this near accident could not wake him, and he fought sleep just to make the next two miles home. The following day Louis gave notice at the truck line. His boss suggested that if his interest was with the restaurant rather than the trucking company, then maybe he should not work out his notice period. Louis agreed.

The following day when Billie asked Louis what time he had to be at work, Louis told her that he had good news and bad news. The good news was that he could spend all of his time helping her in the restaurant; the bad news was that there would be no more steady paychecks. They both knew they had some rocky roads ahead of them. Over the next several months while the restaurant was struggling to make a profit, Louis and Billie learned that restaurant bills and employees get paid first—if anyone went without a paycheck it had to be them. They also learned that they could live at home without electricity for a few days, but the restaurant couldn't. The same went for gas and telephone service.

Slowly, the business began to show a profit. This small restaurant in Social Circle, Georgia, had begun to attract customers from Atlanta, 45 miles away. After being open for eighteen months, the 68 seats in the restaurant could no longer accommodate the business, but there was no way to add on to the restaurant because there was no place to park any additional cars. Meanwhile, a restaurant in Covington, ten miles from Social Circle, closed due to poor business. This 220 seat restaurant had previously been a chain steak house and a family restaurant. In late April 1987 Louis and Billie closed Billie's Classic Country Dining and opened Billie's Family Restaurant in Covington, Georgia. From the beginning business was good. Although the Van Dykes lost a lot of their Atlanta customers who came for the small town atmosphere and the setting of the old country cottage in Social Circle, the restaurant was now in an area with ten times the population of Social Circle. The restaurant developed a reputation for excellent Southern cooking served buffet style, and business was booming.

The good fortune was short lived, however; the building that housed the restaurant was in very poor condition. Termite infestations closed the restaurant the first time termites swarmed and ruined the food. When it rained, over three-fourths of the dining room had to be closed due to a leaking roof. Utility bills were tremendous due to poor construction planning when the building was built. After eighteen months in a deteriorating facility with escalating costs, the Van Dykes closed Billie's Family Restaurant in Covington. All efforts to have the property owner maintain the roof and building had failed.

Several months prior to closing the Covington restaurant, The American Legion Post in Monroe, Georgia, contacted Louis and Billie and asked them to operate the restaurant in the American Legion Hall originally established in the 1950s. The restaurant there had fallen on hard times, and the current operator had decided not to renew the lease. The commander of the American Legion made an offer too attractive for Louis and Billie to refuse, and in September of 1987 they opened Billie's at the American Legion. While Louis ran the day-to-day operation at the Covington restaurant, Billie and their son Chip ran the restaurant in Monroe. After they closed the Covington restaurant, Louis joined Billie in the Monroe restaurant and ran the kitchen as head cook while Billie handled the dining room.

What had been a floundering restaurant serving only thirty to thirty-five meals at lunch Monday through Friday and only fifty to sixty people on Sundays was soon serving over two hundred people for lunch daily during the week and up to five hundred people on Sundays. At nights and on weekends, the facility stayed busy with banquets, parties, wedding receptions and other catered events. It was during this time that the Blue Willow dream began to come true.

From the time that the Van Dykes moved from the crowded confines of Atlanta to their land outside of Social Circle, they had admired the grand, yet dilapidated, old mansion in Social

Circle formerly known as the Bertha Upshaw Clubhouse. A few of the older homes in Social Circle were in varying degrees of disrepair, but the mansion that was eventually to become the Blue Willow Inn Restaurant was abandoned and seriously neglected. After inquiring among the locals, Billie and Louis discovered that the mansion had at one time been the center of civic and cultural activity in Social Circle, but the property had fallen on hard times in the late 1960s during desegregation. During the 1950s the city had built a swimming pool on the property, but when integration came to the clubhouse and the swimming pool, the various clubs in Social Circle sadly abandoned the property. The result was lawsuits for control of the property, and the issue of ownership remained in the courts until 1985 when the Georgia Supreme Court ruled that the property was to revert back to the estate of the original owners, the Upshaw family.

While the Van Dykes were struggling to make their first restaurant a success, Billie and Louis dreamed of one day owning this grand old mansion just three blocks away. Of course, they knew this was just a dream. While struggling to keep the doors open in the small cottage restaurant, how could they possibly ever have the means to purchase and restore such a place?

One day during lunch at the restaurant, Billie met Reverend and Mrs. Homer Harvey. The Harveys told Billie how much they enjoyed their lunch and that they would soon become regular customers. Reverend Harvey, a Church of God minister, then told Billie that he had just purchased the Bertha Upshaw Clubhouse and was starting the Social Circle Church of God in the old mansion. Billie replied, "You mean the old house I've always wanted?" Reverend Harvey was not sure it was the same house, but Billie knew that it was.

Even after closing the restaurant in Social Circle, moving to Covington, and opening the restaurant in Monroe, Billie still dreamed of one day owning the old mansion she loved, all the while knowing it was just a dream. Soon Louis and Billie found themselves going to fundraising dinners and yard sales at the church just to see the inside of the mansion. Each time Billie was in the old house, she would mentally design a restaurant layout inside the house and fancy herself opening the massive front door to customers and guests.

While Billie was at a spaghetti supper hosted by the ladies of the church, Reverend Harvey mentioned to her that the house would make a nice restaurant. "Don't tease me!" Billie exclaimed. "We're not teasing," replied Pastor Harvey. "We wanted to restore this old house, but . . . we're just getting too old. We plan to sell the mansion when we finish the new church on the back of the property." Billie was elated. She could barely wait until Louis got home from the restaurant in Monroe so that she could share the news.

"Reverend Harvey is selling the mansion, and he said we could purchase it for a restaurant!" Billie excitedly told Louis as he pulled into their driveway at home. Louis told Billie not to tease him and said, "We can't afford it anyway. What would we do for money?" Billie would not give up this easily, however, and she insisted that Louis go to the bank and try to borrow the money. Over Louis's protests that they had finally finished paying off the losses at the Covington restaurant and had very little money, Billie insisted that he at least try.

Several days later as Billie was mentally placing tables, furnishings and a kitchen in the mansion, Louis told her that he had gone to the bank for financing to purchase the mansion that Reverend Harvey had agreed to sell to them for around $200,000. Louis shared the bad news with Billie that the banker had responded, "You want to do what with our money? Where? You must be kidding! You'll never serve enough meals in Social Circle to pay for the purchase much less the repairs!" Louis took this as a no.

That was 1990. Louis and Billie had struggled, made mistakes, paid off losses and still had a dream. The restaurant at the American Legion in Monroe was successful, but the dining room was a large cafeteria style dining hall. They both missed the charm and decor of their first restaurant, the small cottage in Social Circle. They both wanted a permanent location in an old house, and they both wanted the old mansion in Social Circle. If there was a way, they would find it.

When Billie told Reverend Harvey that the bank had turned Louis down flat, he told her that he might consider financing the purchase. When she told him that they did not have the money to make a down payment on a purchase that size, Pastor Harvey told her that he would finance one hundred percent of the purchase price. Billie was ecstatic!

As soon as Billie saw Louis, she shared this good news, but Louis was hesitant. Although the Harveys had partially restored the old mansion, finishing the repairs, adding a kitchen, rewiring, and redecorating would cost a lot of money; the whole project seemed overwhelming. "Restorations like this take tens of thousands of dollars," Louis thought out loud. "We can do it," Billie countered. "We'll take extra parties and banquets at the restaurant in Monroe and we'll do more catering. With the extra money, we can buy supplies and materials and do the work ourselves." They both agreed that this was an almost overwhelming project without bank financing. It was time for prayer.

When Louis opened the restaurant in Covington, everything went great. Money was coming in and for the first time since opening the first restaurant, the Van Dykes had a cash reserve, but Louis wanted more—he wanted to get rich and open more restaurants. He had taken the business out of God's care and decided he could do it on his own. Louis thought: *What a fool I was. Since the 1970s I had depended on the Lord for guid-*

ance and leading. I walked away from Him and decided I would get rich, but I learned a lesson from God. If it could go wrong at the Covington restaurant, it would and did go wrong. After closing the restaurant in Covington, Louis realized that he had just learned a hard lesson. He lost his desire to get rich and as a result, he would not make a decision about the old mansion until he had prayed and sought God. For Billie, seeking God's will was a part of her daily life, but for Louis, it was part of a roller coaster ride with God.

Louis and Billie both agreed that they needed a word from the Lord before signing the papers to purchase the mansion, so they both went to prayer. The day before they were to sign the papers, they still had no answers to their prayers. After agreeing together that perhaps it was not time to pursue their dream, Louis began to read the Bible. The Lord answered that prayer with the scripture Isaiah Chapter 44, verses 8 and 9, which reads, "Fear ye not, neither be afraid: have not I told thee from that time, and have declared it; ye are even my witnesses. Is there a God beside me? Yea, there is no God; I know not any. They that make a graven image are all of them vanity: and their delectable things shall not profit; and they are their own witnesses; they see not, nor know; that they may be ashamed." After sharing this scripture with Billie, they both agreed that this was a powerful word from the Lord and that they had best not make the new restaurant their god. Louis did not want to learn the same lesson twice.

After receiving this confirmation, with the warning to keep their priorities straight, Louis and Billie had peace about their decision and signed the papers to purchase their dream in the summer of 1990. They decided to place their home up for sale in order to help finance the renovations. Almost overnight they had a signed contract to sell their house, but the Gulf War crisis caused the housing market to collapse. The Van Dykes were still confident that their house would sell giving them the money for renovations. The mansion was large enough that they could live on the second floor while operating the restaurant on the first floor.

After getting the proper zoning to operate a restaurant in the house, the hard work began. Every free hour for ten months was spent scraping paint, replacing wiring, installing plumbing, and finishing floors. With the help of family and friends, the Van Dykes worked around the clock and spent several sleepless nights before the Blue Willow Inn Restaurant opened on Thanksgiving Day 1991, and what a day it was.

In order to save money, the Van Dykes had purchased used kitchen equipment which decided to rebel on Thanksgiving Day; if anything could go wrong that day, it did. With a lot of improvising and patching, they got through their first day, but Louis and Billie still advise never to open a new restaurant on Thanksgiving Day.

With the opening of the Blue Willow Inn Restaurant behind them, Louis and Billie concentrated on finishing the renovations of the Blue Willow Inn and operating both restaurants. They knew that they had only a few months left on the lease at the American Legion restaurant in Monroe. They also knew that the lease would not be renewed as the new officers of the American Legion had indicated that they wanted to close the restaurant and turn it into a dance hall and bingo parlor. Although a year was left on their lease, the Van Dykes agreed to terminate the lease six months early after experiencing three arson attempts and a break-in during which acid was poured into their cash register and all of their food was contaminated with lamp oil. By the time the Monroe restaurant was closed in June of 1992, the Blue Willow Inn Restaurant had finally become profitable, but not without some rough times getting there.

By January 1992, the Van Dykes were experiencing serious financial problems. While the restaurant in Monroe was operating profitably in spite of the break-ins and fires, the Blue Willow Inn had a mountain of start-up bills that remained unpaid. With the

Gulf War housing market collapse, their house never sold. Their lawyer and accountant both told them that they should consider bankruptcy, but Louis and Billie had been in tight spots before and did not consider bankruptcy an option. Somehow, they would make it work.

On March 9, 1992, Louis had gotten some particularly bad news, and that night as he and Billie exhaustibly prepared to get some sleep, Louis roared, "Life's lousy! I wish I were dead!" As Louis slept, Billie stayed awake all night praying. She prayed, "Louis and I have worked hard and are trying to follow Your will. I have prayed for miracles for others before but have never prayed for a miracle for myself. But," Billie told the Lord, "we need a miracle."

The following evening, a writer named Marty Godbey was dining at the Blue Willow Inn, and she asked to meet the owners. After she introduced herself to Billie and Louis, she told them that she was writing a book entitled *Dining in Historic Georgia.* She told them that she had previously dined at the Blue Willow Inn and had decided to include the Blue Willow Inn in her book. Billie and Louis were both very pleased and proud to be a part of the few select restaurants that would be featured in the book. Louis thought to himself: *This is nice, but by the time the book is out the Blue Willow Inn may be history.* As it turns out, by the time the book was published, the Blue Willow Inn was not history, but was featured on the cover of the book.

On the following day, Wednesday, March 11, 1992, while Louis was cooking in the kitchen at the Blue Willow Inn, a friend and customer, Elton Wright, came into the kitchen with good news. "Lewis Grizzard is dining with you today!" he exclaimed. Louis was excited; he had recently read one of Mr. Grizzard's columns criticizing a Southern restaurant in Atlanta, which in addition to its other Southern cooking misdeeds had served mashed potatoes out of a box! Having read all of Lewis Grizzard's books, Louis knew that he was always searching for just the right restaurant with authentic Southern cooking.

When Louis went to the dining room to welcome Mr. Grizzard to the Blue Willow Inn, he found the columnist sitting in front of a heaping plate of food. While eating the entire time he and Louis were talking, Mr. Grizzard heaped praises on the food, particularly the fried green tomatoes. Remembering Mr. Grizzard's comments about mashed potatoes coming out of a box, Louis moaned inwardly as he realized that he did not have mashed potatoes on the buffet line that day. Then Louis remembered that he had a bowl of leftover mashed potatoes from the day before, which he quickly heated and served to Mr. Grizzard. When Mr. Grizzard finished his lunch, he complimented the food and said, "Watch the paper." Louis could barely contain himself. Some of his customers and most of his staff thought he had lost his mind while he jumped, hooted, and hollered for the next few minutes.

That night when Louis and Billie were discussing Mr. Grizzard's visit to the Blue Willow Inn, Billie was secretly disappointed. She had prayed for a miracle. She had expected someone to walk up to her or Louis with a check; she had not expected Lewis Grizzard, but nevertheless, Lewis Grizzard was their miracle. On the following Friday in the *Atlanta Journal* newspaper, Lewis Grizzard's column featured the Blue Willow Inn Restaurant and their fried green tomatoes. Mr. Grizzard ended his column with the following:

> I am a connoisseur of authentic Southern cooking, which is getting more and more difficult to locate. Half the time you think you've stumbled upon it, they serve mashed potatoes that come out of a box.
> But not at the Blue Willow Inn in Social Circle.
> If I gave ratings for Southern cooking, I'd have to give the Blue Willow my absolute highest mark—5 bowls of turnip greens.

Every dish was authentic and delicious, including the banana pudding I had for dessert.

I shall return.

Unfortunately, return he didn't. Shortly after writing the column, Mr. Grizzard began to suffer problems with his heart. The Van Dykes enclosed and extended one of the side porches to expand the seating. Although Mr. Grizzard gave permission to name the new room the "Lewis Grizzard Room" in his honor, his health did not allow him to return to dedicate the room.

The Grizzard column was syndicated in almost three hundred newspapers throughout the country. The Van Dykes got phone calls, visitors and letters from all over the country as a result of the column, and that weekend they made their first profit since opening the Blue Willow Inn Restaurant. Lewis Grizzard may never have known it, but he was their miracle. All of the start-up bills were paid off in just a matter of weeks.

Since that time, the Blue Willow Inn and the Van Dykes have been featured in magazines such as *Southern Living, Gourmet,* and *A Taste of Home* and on such television shows as Cable News Network's travel show and cooking show. In June of 1996, *Guideposts* magazine featured Billie in a story entitled "The Inn of My Dreams." In the spring of 1996, the Blue Willow Inn Restaurant was awarded *Southern Living* magazine's Readers' Choice Award for Best Small Town Restaurant in the South.

Having served guests from all 50 states and from over 150 foreign countries, the Blue Willow Inn has established itself as one of the South's premier restaurants—all as the result of a dream, hard work, a miracle and the blessings of the Lord.

EXPERIENCING TRADITIONAL SOUTHERN COOKING AND HOSPITALITY: A BRIEF HISTORY

Visitors to the Blue Willow Inn Restaurant in Social Circle, Georgia, frequently ask us why Southerners act the way they do, talk the way they do, and cook the way they do—and why they do all of these things so *slowly*. Perhaps not even the most learned scholars of Southern culture can answer these questions with certainty, but the fact remains that Southerners are known for their hospitable treatment of visitors and friends, their slow pace of life, their manner of talking, and their delicious style of cooking. Although few can explain the Southern hospitality phenomenon, few would deny its existence. It is common in areas such as Social Circle, Georgia, to hear a visitor from another state or country remark that Southern hospitality is truly alive and well today.

For example, after the 1996 Olympic Games were held in Atlanta, Georgia, even after media reports of traffic congestion and scheduling problems, visitors to Atlanta could be overheard marveling at hospitable acts from Native Georgians rather than complaining about the crowds or the heat. One man was overheard recounting the tale of an Atlanta resident loaning his cellular phone to someone in the crowd in desperate need to contact the rest of his party. Another was heard boasting of a young woman allowing a family with small children to board the already crowded MARTA (Atlanta mass transit) train ahead of her. Although these examples of Southern hospitality boast a modern age twist of mobile phones and mass transit systems, Southern hospitality is not a myth perpetrated by the Hollywood version of life in the South—it is a reality and a way of life for most Southerners.

Some speculate that this way of life (and it is a way of life, not merely an attitude to exhibit on special occasions or for special company) is a function of the Southern colonies traditionally being more rural and agricultural. In rural societies people had to travel quite a distance to visit with one another and stayed for a while once they arrived at their destination.

Others speculate that the impeccable manners of Southern inhabitants were simply passed down from the original settlers of the area, chiefly the English and the French, two cultures known for their code of manners. English colonists began the establishment of Jamestown in 1607, which by 1700 had grown into a colony of 70,000 settlers. In addition, in 1670, English colonists established the first European colony in the Low Country, which eventually came to be called Charleston. Not long after this, the Low Country was settled by immigrants from Barbados and the French Huguenots.

The hospitality and manners of the Old South are alive and well in the Modern South. For example, studies have shown that most Southern parents teach their children to address adults as "Ma'am" and "Sir." In addition, studies have also shown that helpful behaviors are more frequent in the South.

Most Southerners and visitors to the South, however, do not need a poll or an empirical study to tell them that hospitality and helpfulness are a natural part of the Southern experience. The comments overheard from those visiting from other regions testify to the surprising fact that friendliness and openness pervade the behavior of Southerners—whether it is the act of holding the door open for someone, taking food to the family of one who is sick or in the hospital, or the modern day kindness of lending someone your cellular phone. To experience this kindness is to experience the South.

A characteristically Southern trait that goes hand-in-hand with hospitality is the trademark slower pace for which the South is known. To experience the South is to experience a pace of life which is less frenetic, patterns of speech which are more melodic, and attitudes which are more relaxed. This slow pace seems to lend itself to the attitude of hospitality; if you are not always in a hurry, you are more likely to offer someone a cold drink, to invite someone in to visit awhile, or to pick up someone's dropped pencil and return it.

Although the pace of life in the South may indeed be slower, Southerners would no doubt emphasize that this slower pace does not mean that they do not work as hard as those in other regions. Harper Lee, author of *To Kill A Mockingbird*, explained away the perception that because Southerners do not move as quickly that they do not work as hard by stating, "We work hard, of course, but we do it in a different way. We work hard in order not to work. Any time spent on business is more or less wasted, but you have to do it in order to be able to hunt and fish and gossip."

In addition to the perception that Southerners move more slowly than others is the perception that Southerners speak more slowly. Surprisingly, studies have shown that Southerners speak nearly as many words per minute as others—they merely draw the words out longer. Novelist Reynolds Price noted that, "Southerners employ more notes of the scale than other Americans; they need them for their broader reach of expression," or as Mark Twain said, "The Southerner talks music." Regardless of the results of empirical studies, many Southerners would beg to differ with the finding that Southerners do not actually talk more slowly but just sound as if they do. Any Southerner who has been to the local drugstore or cafe and for the fourth time that week has patiently listened to Junior explain how he reeled in the ten pound ornery catfish from Lake Hoosawatchie would no doubt firmly insist that Southerners do, in fact, speak more slowly.

The manner of Southern speech patterns are not as controversial—most everyone would agree that Southerners have speech patterns and vocabulary peculiar to the South. Not only do Southerners use different words, but they pronounce the same words differently. For example, Southerners frequently omit the *r* sound when it follows a vowel, so that *pardon* becomes *pahden* and *butter* becomes *buddah*. Mark Twain remarked that "the educated Southerner has no use for an r, except at the beginning of a word."

Contrary to the belief of some, pure Elizabethan English has not been preserved in areas of the South. Linguists believe, however, that the speech patterns of the Lower South resemble that of London and counties of Southern England, while the speech patterns of the Upper South resemble that of Northern England, Scotland, and Northern Ireland.

Other cultures have contributed to our present day Southern vocabulary. For example, the phrase most commonly linked with the South, "you all" or "y'all" appears to be a modern day replacement for the second-person plural no longer present in the English language, which is why Southerners become so offended when non-Southerners attempt to poke fun at Southerners and misuse the term by referring to one person, when any self-respecting Southerner knows that you only use "y'all" when speaking to more than one person. African contributions to the present day Southern vocabulary include *banjo and okra.*

Another term peculiar to the South is the use of "dinner" to mean the midday meal, which was the main meal of the day in agricultural societies such as the South. The evening meal was often much lighter and was dubbed "supper." Although the practice of eating the heavier meal at noon has all but vanished, except on Sundays, Southerners still often refer to a noonday meal as *dinner* and an evening meal as *supper.*

One thing is for certain—whether Southerners are eating dinner or supper—they enjoy a cuisine and a style of cooking native to the South and for which the South is famous. A definition of what makes food Southern requires some explaining because Southern food is different things to different people. To some it is bending over vines on hot August days picking the peas, okra and squash that will grace the table on cold winter nights. To some it is sitting on a front porch in the cool of the evening shelling those same peas and passing the time with family and loved ones. To some it is the first real tomato sandwich of summer—the one with the first tomato vine ripe and pulled by hand—heavy on the salt, pepper, and mayonnaise. To some the term conjures up notions of elegant restaurants in Charleston, New Orleans, and Savannah—places with white linen napkins and sterling silver tableware. To others it is paper plates and sawdust floors and barbecue sauce dripping down the chin. Still others hear Southern food and think of slices of ice cold watermelon or ice cream made in an oak bucket and churned by hand. Others recall platters of crisp fried chicken, served only for company. Sadly, there are people in the world who have no notion whatsoever of true Southern cooking.

Although Southern food conjures up different images, down-home Southern cuisine traditionally uses what Southern farms have historically and can easily produce. Thus, corn and pork, two products easily cultivated in the Southern climate, have served as the mainstay of Southern cuisine. Pork has been the meat of choice (or at least availability) in the South since well before the Civil War. History shows that hogs came to Jamestown with the first English settlers, then traveled across the South with the pioneers. Pork soon became a staple to both high and low southern cuisine; almost every part of the hog was used—meat was eaten, lard was used for cooking, lighting, soap and ointments. Raising hogs was relatively easy, as farmers could either turn the hogs loose to forage the land to eat until they were ready for slaughter or feed the hogs on corn, a crop indigenous to the South and also a crucial element of Southern cooking.

Corn was already being grown by Southern Native Americans when the colonists first arrived, and this crop they called "maize" soon became a mainstay for Southern hogs, horses, mules, and people. Even after the Civil War, Southern households purchased two and a half times more cornmeal than other Americans. Corn, although delicious on the cob, takes many forms in Southern cooking—hominy, grits, cornmeal, cornbread, hushpuppies, and much to the prohibitionist's dismay—corn whiskey and bourbon.

Native Americans also provided Southerners with a popular delicacy, one for which the Blue Willow Inn is famous—fried green tomatoes. Native Americans are said to have introduced this dish to colonists who were so taken by the dish that they exported it to Europe as early as the 1500s. The Catholic Church banned eating red ripe tomatoes because the texture of a ripe tomato's skin was similar to the texture of the human skin, and thus, the red tomato was considered an aphrodisiac. When the tomatoes were in season, however, you can bet that more than a few of even the most devout individuals hid in armoires or pulled the curtains shut in order to delight in the forbidden fruit. The consumption of green tomatoes was permitted, however, which may be one of the reasons that the most popular type of tomatoes used for this dish is the green tomato. The earliest recorded history of fried green tomatoes is in Northern Italy, and the cook probably used olive oil for frying them.

In addition to corn and fresh vegetables such as tomatoes, other staples of the Southern kitchen include other meats and crops easily obtained or grown. For example, poultry, game and catfish were and are popular meats used in Southern cooking. Other crops grown easily in the Southern climate are black eyed peas, greens, okra, rice, tomatoes, Vidalia onions (grown in and around Vidalia, Georgia, where the soil makes them sweet as molasses), and watermelon.

The method for preparing these foods is similar to the nature of the foods themselves—Southerners have traditionally used the ingredients on hand to enhance the staples on hand. For example, a traditional Southern method of cooking is to deep fry everything from catfish to sliced green tomatoes—the lard and cornmeal are an ever present help to combat a tiresome menu. Novelist Reynolds Price described the Southern lunch as "chicken and cured ham, corn pudding, green beans, spring onions, tomatoes, small limas, hot rolls, corn sticks, iced tea, and lemon pie (with all the ingredients but the tea and lemons grown no more than twenty miles off)."

Recently a new phenomenon known as "New Southern Cuisine" has been popping up around the South in an attempt to lighten the traditionally high calorie Southern dishes while incorporating ingredients not traditionally used in Southern cooking. This new Southern cooking style has been extolled and practiced in many modern Southern cookbooks and trendy restaurants. Whether you prefer traditional "down home" Southern cuisine or the new South recipes, it is probable that the notion of Southern cuisine—old or new—cannot be easily defined and conjures up different images to different folks.

To some it is catfish and grits and sweet iced tea. To others it is fried and seasoned with something that came from a hog. It is garden fresh or readily available without traveling north of Richmond. It is made with crab and served with rice in the Carolina low country. It is shrimp and fish along the Georgia coast; crayfish from the Bayou in Louisiana, cured ham in Kentucky and Virginia, red-eye gravy in Tennessee, and fried chicken and okra anywhere below the Mason-Dixon line. Southern food is turnip greens, peas, and collards, seasoned with just the right amount of fatback and pot likker and pepper sauce and cornbread for sopping. It is barbecue that doesn't involve beef and biscuits that have never been trapped inside a can, served hot with real butter.

Southern food, whatever the definition, was not created; it has evolved. It epitomizes the Southern spirit in that Southerners have always taken what they might have on hand and gone well beyond making do—turning very modest fare into delec table culinary treasures. It is served with pride and eaten with great relish. It adds joy to any celebration, absorbs tears better than a sponge and is usually the very first thing offered when Southerners need to help one another deal with grief.

Recipes of Southern dishes have been passed down from generation to generation, changing with the times when necessary, adapted and improved upon. Some foods have even been glamorized to the point of legend. Sadly, many Southern recipes have been changed drastically to suit our modern lifestyle of hurry, hurry, hurry, not to mention the nineties notion that anything that tastes good must be bad for you. Many Southerners have lost the art of preparing fresh food from scratch, seasoning it with just the right combination of salt, pork, and butter, and serving it up hot in enormous helpings to grateful crowds of hungry family and friends. New generations of children in the South are growing up without knowing the joy of sitting down to a scrumptious meal of true Southern victuals. The old recipes are not being passed down and yet another part of our heritage may soon be gone with the same wind that is sweeping away so many other facets of our culture.

We are dedicated at the Blue Willow Inn to serving authentic Southern dishes, prepared in the same manner in which they have been prepared for generations—with a few special touches belonging only to us. It is always our hope that our customers will experience Southern hospitality and charm at its best and leave fully satisfied and eager to visit again. By publishing these recipes, we hope to pass along a little bit of the Southern culture to future generations and to enable people from all areas to open this cookbook, experiment with these delicious recipes and . . . experience the South.

John Lowe and his mother Gertrude are two of the Blue Willow Inn's most faithful customers. They drive down from Cornelia, Georgia (which is 1 1/2 hours each way) twice a week to dine at the restaurant. John's Quail recipe can be found on page 163.

EXPERIENCING
APPETIZERS

Visitors to the Blue Willow Inn Restaurant *are greeted by Southern Belles adorned in antebellum garb who make every effort to ensure that your experience at the Blue Willow Inn is an experience in Southern Hospitality.*

43

Deviled Eggs

Every Southern hostess knows the importance of preparing deviled eggs, and protocol dictates that a true Southern lady own a deviled egg dish. No luncheon in the South is complete without deviled eggs.

7	hard-boiled eggs
2	tablespoons mayonnaise
½	teaspoons prepared mustard, optional
1	tablespoon sweet pickle relish, optional
	salt and pepper to taste
	fresh parsley for garnish
	black or green olives for garnish
	paprika, optional

- Peel hard-boiled eggs.
- Cut 6 eggs in half lengthwise. Remove yolks from cut eggs.
- Combine yolks, mayonnaise, mustard, pickle relish, salt and pepper.
- Mix well with a fork to mash eggs and yolks.
- Either pipe or spoon filling into egg cavities.
- Garnish each egg with a green or black olive half and parsley sprig.
- If desired, sprinkle with a small amount of paprika before garnishing.
- Serve in deviled egg dish.

Yield: 6 servings.

WONDERFULLY SOUTHERN!
--JERSEY CITY, NEW JERSEY

Spinach Balls

2	packages frozen chopped spinach
1	tablespoon black pepper
5	eggs, beaten
½	cup grated Parmesan cheese
1	stick melted butter
1	medium chopped onion
1	package chicken flavored Stove Top stuffing

- Cook the spinach and drain.
- Combine all ingredients in a mixing bowl and mix well.
- Form into walnut size balls.
- Bake at 325 degrees for 20 minutes on a sheet pan.
  Yield: 50-60 balls.

Shrimp Wrapped in Bacon

desired amount of shrimp
equal number of pieces of bacon
French salad dressing

- Peel and clean the shrimp.
- Marinate for 2 hours in French dressing.
- Wrap with bacon and fasten bacon with a toothpick.
- Bake at 350 degrees on a shallow baking pan for 20 minutes, turning once.
- Drain on paper towel.

BACON-CHESTNUT APPETIZERS

15   slices bacon
1   cup water chestnuts

☕ Cut bacon lengthwise and wrap around water chestnuts.
☕ Bake at 350 degrees for 25-30 minutes, turning once.
☕ Drain on paper towel.

SAUSAGE BALLS IN CHEESE PASTRY

*These can be prepared ahead and frozen. Simply reheat
on low heat in oven.*

1   pound mild or hot bulk pork sausages
¾   cup dry bread crumbs
⅓   cup chicken broth
⅛   teaspoon ground nutmeg
¼   teaspoon poultry seasoning
1 ½   cups all-purpose flour
¼   teaspoon salt
1   teaspoon paprika
2   cups sharp Cheddar cheese, shredded
½   cup butter, softened

☕ Combine first five ingredients, mixing well.
☕ Shape into 1-inch balls.
☕ Bake at 300 degrees until brown.
☕ Drain on paper towels.
☕ Combine flour, salt, paprika and cheese.
☕ Cut in butter with pastry blender. Mix with hands until smooth.

- Shape 1 tablespoon of dough around each sausage ball covering ball completely.
- Place on greased baking pan and bake at 350 degrees for 15-20 minutes until golden brown.

Yield: 4 dozen

BACON ROLL UPS

¼	**cup butter**
½	**cup water**
1 ½	**cups herb-seasoned bread stuffing crumbs**
1	**egg, slightly beaten**
¼	**pound bulk hot or mild pork sausages**
⅔	**pound bacon**

- In saucepan melt butter in water.
- Remove butter mixture from heat and stir into stuffing.
- Add egg and sausage and blend thoroughly.
- Chill for one hour and remove from refrigeration and shape into balls resembling pecans.
- Cut bacon into thirds and wrap the balls with bacon and secure with a toothpick.
- Bake at 375 degrees for 35-40 minutes in a shallow baking pan turning once.
- Drain on paper towels.
- Serve hot.

Yield: 3 dozen

47

SWEET AND SOUR MEATBALLS
These can be made a day ahead.

2	pounds ground beef
2	eggs, slightly beaten
½	cup bread crumbs
½	cup water
1	12-ounce bottle Heinz chili sauce
1	16-ounce jar grape jelly
	salt and pepper to taste
	garlic powder to taste

- Combine ground beef, eggs, bread crumbs, water, salt, pepper and garlic powder.
- Shape into walnut size balls.
- Cook for 15-20 minutes on ungreased baking pan at 350 degrees until lightly browned.
- Drain.
- In a small saucepan combine chili sauce, grape jelly and lemon.
- Bring to a slow boil.
- Add cooked meatballs and allow to simmer for 8-10 minutes.
- Serve hot in a chafing dish.

Yield: about 4 dozen.

CHEESE COOKIES
This recipe was Petra Broberg's.

3	cups plain flour
½	cup chopped nuts

2   sticks butter
1   pound Kraft Longhorn or sharp Cheddar cheese
1   cup pecan halves
      dash cayenne pepper

- Mix all ingredients.
- On a lightly floured surface shape into a roll about the diameter of a quarter.
- Chill.
- Slice and place on an ungreased sheet pan ⅛-inch apart.
- Place one pecan half in the center of each cookie.
- Bake at 350 degrees for 10-12 minutes. Do not brown.
  NOTE: These freeze well. Freeze in a tight tin with waxed paper between each layer.
  Yield: about 125 bite size cookies.

MEAT AND CHEESE TRAY

1   pound thin sliced roast beef
1   pound thin sliced ham
1   pound thin sliced smoked turkey breast
½   pound thin sliced Swiss cheese
½   pound thin sliced American cheese
16   assorted hard rolls
6   ounces mayonnaise
2   ounces Dijon mustard
      fancy leaf lettuce

- Arrange the lettuce to cover 12-14-inch round platter.
- Mix mayonnaise and mustard together.
- Place in a small bowl in center of platter. (Cont.→)

- Arrange the meats and cheeses around perimeter of platter.
- Place assorted rolls in basket.
  Yield: 12-16 servings.

STUFFED CHERRY TOMATOES

This is both a colorful and tasty dish to serve with finger foods.

**desired number of cherry tomatoes
shrimp salad, tuna salad or chicken salad
fancy leaf lettuce**

- Wash the cherry tomatoes.
- Hull out the centers of cherry tomatoes and discard centers.
- With a pastry bag or spoon, fill the centers of the tomatoes with your favorite prepared salad.
- To serve, cover serving dish or tray with fancy leaf lettuce.
- If tomatoes will not stay upright on tray, square off the bottom of the tomatoes with a sharp knife removing only enough to stay upright.

SPICED OLIVES

2	**cups large pitted green olives**
½	**cup liquid from olives**
⅓	**cup olive oil**
1	**tablespoon minced garlic**
½	**teaspoon crushed oregano**

Combine olive liquid with oil, garlic and oregano.

Place olives into container and cover with liquid.

Cover and refrigerate 24 hours before serving.

GRANNY SMITH APPLES WITH CARAMEL FONDUE

If possible, apples should be cut immediately prior to serving to prevent browning. If apples are not served immediately, place apple slices in cold water with small amount of lemon juice. Caramel fondue can be prepared ahead and refrigerated. Simply reheat before serving.

12-15   pieces ½-ounce caramel candy
1   small can Eagle Brand sweetened condensed milk
8   Granny Smith apples

Place caramel candy in a microwave safe bowl.

Microwave over medium heat until melted stirring 2-3 times while melting.

Remove from microwave oven and add sweetened condensed milk.

Stir to mix well.

Place back in microwave long enough to blend caramel and condensed milk, stirring two to three times.

Wash and slice apples and arrange apple slices on a tray with a chafing dish or fondue dish in center.

Place caramel mix in chafing dish or fondue dish over medium heat.

> LIKE *GONE WITH THE WIND*!
> --MILFORD, CONNECTICUT

SUGARED NUTS

This recipe was submitted by Margaret Hale.

2 ½   **cups pecan halves**
½   **cup water**
1   **cup sugar**
1   **teaspoon cinnamon**
1   **teaspoon salt**

- Heat the pecans in a 375 degree oven for 15 minutes.
- Cook other ingredients to soft boil stage without stirring.
- Add the nuts and mix.
- Pour onto waxed paper and separate immediately.
- Cool before serving.

CHEX PARTY MIX

This is the traditional mix. Although party mixes can now be purchased in the grocery store, none of them are the same as the traditional mixes prepared in home kitchens.

1   **stick butter or margarine**
1 ¼   **teaspoons seasoned salt**
4 ½   **teaspoons Worcestershire sauce**
2 ⅔   **cups Corn Chex cereal**
2 ⅔   **cups Rice Chex cereal**
2 ⅔   **cups Wheat Chex cereal**
1   **cup salted mixed nuts**

- Preheat oven to 350 degrees.
- Heat margarine in large shallow roasting pan (about 15x10x2-inch) in oven until melted.

- Remove from oven.
- Stir in seasoned salt and Worcestershire sauce.
- Add Chex cereals and nuts.
- Mix until all pieces are coated.
- Heat in oven 350 degrees 1 hour, stirring every 15 minutes.
- Spread on paper towel to cool.

MICROWAVE DIRECTIONS:

- In a large microwavable bowl melt butter on high for 1 minute.
- Stir in seasoned salt and Worcestershire sauce.
- Add Chex cereals and nuts.
- Mix until all pieces are coated.
- Microwave on high for 6-7 minutes, stirring every 2 minutes.

Yield: 9 cups

PEA-CHOC

This recipe was given to us by Lynn Kelley. Lynn's husband is our produce supplier. She fixes this for her children, and they love it. A good snack item for children of all ages.

1 **cup peanut butter**
1 **cup Nestle's chocolate milk mix**
¼ **cup milk**

- Combine all ingredients and mix well.
- For variety add M&M's, peanuts, graham cracker crumbs, minimarshmallows, or Rice Krispies and mix well.
- This is to be eaten with a spoon.

Yield: 4 servings.

53

CHEESE MOLD

This cheese mold serves well as an appetizer before a meal or as one of several hors d'oeuvres at stand-up receptions. Complements both alcoholic and nonalcoholic beverages.

1½	**pounds grated sharp Cheddar cheese**
3	**8-ounce packages cream cheese, softened**
1	**small finely chopped onion**
3	**drops Tabasco sauce**
1	**cup finely chopped pecans**
	strawberry preserves
	Ritz crackers

- Allow cheese and cream cheese to come to room temperature.
- In a large mixing bowl combine Cheddar cheese, cream cheese, onions, Tabasco sauce and chopped pecans.
- Work together using your hands. The heat from your hands should soften the cheeses and allow them to blend together.
- The mixture can then be pressed into a mold.
- Either lightly grease the mold or cover the inside of the mold with plastic wrap.
- When pressing the mixture into the mold, be sure to press into all cavities.
- Chill.
- Remove from mold and pour desired amount of strawberry preserves over top.
- Serve with Ritz crackers.

NOTE: This cheese can be made ahead and frozen. Also, the sides of the cheese mold can be garnished with coarsely chopped pecans pressed into the sides.

SHRIMP MOLD

Make a day ahead so mold can season, then serve with crackers.

1	pound cooked shrimp
2	cups mayonnaise
1	small onion, grated
2	tablespoons horseradish
2	envelopes of unflavored gelatin
½	cup water
	few drops of red coloring to make mixture light pink
	juice of one lemon

- Sprinkle gelatin in water and place in double boiler to dissolve.
- Combine with the remaining ingredients.
- Pour into mold.
- Chill.

HOT BEEF DIP

¼	cup chopped onions
1	tablespoon margarine
1	8-ounce package cream cheese, cubed
1	tablespoon chopped parsley
1	4-ounce can mushrooms, drained
1	2½-ounce package chipped smoked beef
½	cup grated Parmesan cheese
1	cup milk

- Saute onion in margarine.
- Add cheese and milk.   (Cont.→)

 Stir over low heat until cheese is melted.

 Add remaining ingredients.

 Heat thoroughly. Serve hot with chips.

CRAB DIP

1	**8-ounce package cream cheese**
3	**tablespoons mayonnaise**
1	**teaspoon Dijon mustard**
¼	**teaspoon salt**
2	**tablespoons dry white wine**
1	**8-ounce can crabmeat, drained and flaked**

 Combine cream cheese, mayonnaise, mustard and salt on top of double boiler over simmering water.

 Stir until smooth and well blended.

 Add wine gradually.

 Add crabmeat.

 Serve hot in chafing or fondue dish with crackers.

OYSTER DIP

2	**8-ounce packages cream cheese, softened**
1	**teaspoon Worcestershire sauce**
2	**teaspoons lemon juice**
1	**cup sour cream**
1	**3½-ounce can smoked oysters**

 Blend the cheese with Worcestershire sauce, lemon juice and sour cream.

 Combine with oysters. Serve with corn chips.

DILL DIP

Use as a vegetable dip or on crackers.

1	cup mayonnaise
1	cup sour cream
1	tablespoon dill weed
1	tablespoon dried onion flakes or chopped green onions
1	tablespoon parsley
¼	teaspoon seasoned salt, according to taste

☕ Mix all ingredients thoroughly.

☕ Chill.

HOT ARTICHOKE DIP

This recipe was submitted by Becky Dally.

1½	cups mayonnaise
1½	cups freshly grated Parmesan cheese, divided
2	cans artichoke hearts, chopped and drained
	garlic powder to taste
	dash Worcestershire sauce

☕ Mix all ingredients and place in a small casserole dish.

☕ Sprinkle with additional grated Parmesan cheese on top.

☕ Bake at 350 degrees for 20 minutes or until bubbly. Serve with party crackers.

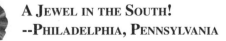

A JEWEL IN THE SOUTH!
--PHILADELPHIA, PENNSYLVANIA

57

GARLIC CHEESE SPREAD
This recipe was submitted by Marie Van Dyke.

2	8-ounce packages cream cheese, softened
10	ounces shredded sharp Cheddar cheese
1	16-ounce jar Cheese Whiz
1	teaspoon fresh minced garlic

In food processor or mixer blend together the cream cheese and Cheese Whiz until smooth.

Add the Cheddar cheese and minced garlic.

Blend until smooth.

Scoop into a serving dish and chill overnight.

Serve with warm french bread.

Yield: 5 cups

CHICKEN LIVER PATE

½	pound chicken livers
2	tablespoons butter
⅓	cup chicken broth
2	hard-boiled eggs
6	ounces softened cream cheese
2	tablespoons dry sherry
	parsley sprigs, optional
	salt and pepper to taste

In a medium skillet saute chicken livers in butter until tender, about 10 minutes.

Stir in broth and swirl in pan.

- Place livers, broth and eggs in blender and blend until smooth. Remove from blender.
- Blend seasonings into cream cheese.
- Place liver and cream cheese mixture in food processor. Add sherry and blend well.
- Place pate in greased mold or bowl and chill.
- Turn out and garnish with parsley.

  NOTE: Plastic wrap can be used to line mold or bowl, which makes turning out the pate easier.

TOMATO CHUTNEY

This is served with every meal at the Blue Willow Inn Restaraunt and is good with fried green tomatoes, green beans, and cooked greens.

1	**14-ounce can tomatoes, whole, chopped, not drained**
1	**cup light brown sugar**
½	**cup granulated sugar**
2	**green bell peppers chopped finely**
1	**medium onion chopped finely**
2	**tablespoons tomato ketchup**
6	**drops Tabasco sauce**
1	**teaspoon black pepper**

- Mix all ingredients in saucepan or small stock pot.
- Bring to a boil.
- Allow to simmer for two hours or until cooked to a thick sauce.

PEACH PRESERVES

8	cups fresh ripe peaches
5	cups sugar
1	cup water

- Peel and cut up the peaches.
- Place in a heavy stock pot and cover with sugar.
- Let sit for 1 hour.
- Add water.
- Place on burner over low heat and bring to a slow simmer.
- Cook for about two hours, stirring often to prevent scorching.
- Remove from heat and refrigerate.
- If canning, spoon peaches into clean canning jars, cover with paraffin wax and seal.

FIG PRESERVES

Goes great with hot biscuits.

fresh ripe figs
sugar
water
lemon juice

- Wash and quarter figs.
- Place figs in a heavy stock pot.
- Cover with sugar. For every pound of figs use 1 ¼ pounds of sugar.
- Add 1 teaspoon of lemon juice for each pound of figs.

 Cook over low to medium heat simmering for 1-2 hours, stirring frequently.

 While cooking, mash mixture with a potato masher or vegetable masher.

 Cool.

 Refrigerate overnight.

CHOW CHOW

This recipe was submitted by Sharlotte Stovall. Chow Chow is good over dried beans, collards or turnip greens.

1	**peck green tomatoes**
10	**large onions**
6	**green hot peppers**
2	**small heads cabbage**
1	**green bell pepper**
1	**red bell pepper**
6	**cups water**
2	**cups salt**
1	**quart vinegar**
2	**cups sugar**

 Wash and chop all vegetables finely.

 Combine water and salt in saucepan and bring to a boil to make brine.

 Pour scalding brine over vegetables.

 Let stand for three hours.

 Combine vinegar and sugar and bring to a boil.

 Drain vegetables and add to vinegar/sugar mixture.

 Simmer for 15 minutes.

 Cool.

Yield: 6-8 pints

CHOW CHOW

This recipe was submitted by Annette Taylor. For spicy chow chow, include jalapeno peppers.

2	**large cabbages**
2	**green bell peppers**
6	**large green tomatoes**
1	**quart vinegar**
2	**cups sugar**

- Grate cabbage, bell peppers and green tomatoes to de sired texture.
- In pot combine vinegar and sugar.
- Bring to a boil.
- Add vegetables and cook for 10 minutes.
- Pour into canning jars while hot and cover with wax and seal.

PEPPER JELLY SPREAD

Easy and quick snack or hors d'oeuvre. For variation, use peach chutney in place of pepper jelly.

1	**small jar green or red pepper jelly**
1	**8-ounce package cream cheese, softened**
	Ritz crackers

- Pour pepper jelly over top of cream cheese.
- Serve with crackers.

CRANBERRY ORANGE RELISH

1	14-ounce can whole cranberry sauce
1	14-ounce can jellied cranberry sauce
8	ounces orange marmalade
16	ounces chopped pecans
1	tablespoon lemon juice

- Mix all ingredients.
- Refrigerate.
- Serve with roasted turkey or baked chicken.

CABBAGE RELISH

This recipe was submitted by Kitty Jacobs, Guidelines, Atlanta.

1	head cabbage
2	cucumbers
1	green or red bell pepper
2	carrots
1	onion, sliced thinly
¾	cup sugar
1	cup cider vinegar
½	cup salad oil
1	teaspoon salt
1	teaspoon celery salt
	garlic salt to taste
	pepper to taste

- Cut cabbage into bite size chunks.
- Peel cucumber and slice thinly. (Cont.→)

63

- Cut pepper into 1-inch long strips.
- Slice thinly or grate carrots.
- Slice onions.
- Mix sugar, vinegar, salad oil and seasonings and pour over vegetables.
- Marinate one day before serving, stirring occasionally.
- Keep refrigerated.

Hot Curried Fruit

1	**8-ounce can sliced peaches in juice**
1	**8-ounce can sliced pears in juice**
8	**ounces sliced apples**
6	**ounces apricots**
6	**ounces cherries without stems**
⅓	**cup butter**
¾	**cup light brown sugar**
2	**teaspoons curry powder**

- Partially drain fruit reserving ½ the juice.
- In a stock pot place reserved juice along with all other ingredients.
- Stir.
- Bring to a boil add fruit and simmer for 30-40 minutes.
- Cool.
- Refrigerate overnight.

Great Southern Food, Y'all!
---Vancouver, British Columbia

BLUEBERRY TOPPING

This recipe was submitted by the Hard Labor Creek Blueberry Farm.

½   cup granulated sugar
½   cup water
⅛   teaspoon salt
1   tablespoon cornstarch
1   cup blueberries
1   tablespoon lemon juice
½   teaspoon fresh lemon peels, grated

- In a small saucepan combine sugar, water, salt, cornstarch and a few blueberries.
- Cook, stirring often until mixture boils and thickens.
- Add blueberries. Heat until again boiling.
- Simmer for 5 minutes.
- Stir in the lemon juice and lemon peel.
- Cool.
  NOTE: Good with ice cream when slightly cooled.

CRANBERRY NUT TOPPING

Good spread on top of Cherry Cheese Pie or ice cream.

1   cup cranberry-orange relish, chilled
½   cup chopped walnuts
1   teaspoon grated orange rind

- Place all ingredients in small bowl and mix.

LEMON SAUCE

The Blue Willow Inn uses this topping on hot ginger bread.

1	**pound granulated sugar**
1½	**teaspoons cornstarch**
⅛	**teaspoon salt**
1	**cup boiling water**
2	**tablespoons melted butter**
1½	**teaspoons lemon juice**
1½	**teaspoons grated lemon rind**
	dash nutmeg

- Combine all the ingredients in saucepan.
- Bring to a boil stirring often.
- Cool.

Yield: 1½ cups.

BLUEBERRY SAUCE

Good with Blueberry Pancakes or Blueberry Banana Nut Bread. Wonderful if served warm!

2	**cups water**
¾	**cup sugar**
¼	**cup cornstarch**
24	**ounces blueberries**

- Combine sugar and water in saucepan and bring to a boil.
- Combine cornstarch with a small amount of water to dissolve. Stir into boiling mixture.
- Cook, stirring until thickened.
- Cool.

Yield: 1 quart.

Bourbon Sauce

Good poured over bread pudding, rice pudding and ice cream. For variety, substitute whiskey for bourbon.

1	**stick butter**
1	**cup sugar**
1	**egg, well beaten**
¼	**cup bourbon**

- Heat butter and sugar in microwave until the sugar is dissolved.
- Add egg and whisk rapidly so that the egg does not scramble.
- Add bourbon and mix.
- Cool.

Dill Sauce

Good with grilled, broiled, or baked fish.

¼	**cup sour cream**
¼	**cup mayonnaise**
1	**tablespoon dill weed**
¼	**tablespoon lemon juice**

- Mix all ingredients well.
- Refrigerate.

Yield: 3-4 servings. For more servings, double the recipe.

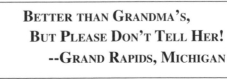

BETTER THAN GRANDMA'S,
BUT PLEASE DON'T TELL HER!
--GRAND RAPIDS, MICHIGAN

CHEESE SAUCE

This is good with Seafood Au Gratin, Ham Potato Casserole and just about any dish calling for cheese sauce. Good poured over steamed broccoli or baked potatoes.

¼	**cup butter, melted**
¼	**cup all-purpose flour**
2	**cups milk**
2½	**cups grated Cheddar cheese**
1	**16-ounce jar Cheese Whiz**
½	**teaspoon salt**
¼	**teaspoon black pepper**

- In a saucepan combine butter and flour.
- Mix well to make a roux.
- Preheat milk in microwave oven if available.
- Add milk to saucepan.
- Heat on medium heat, stirring often to prevent scorching.
- When milk is hot, add Cheese Whiz and grated Cheddar cheese.
- Continue to heat to melt cheeses and blend.
- Add salt and pepper.
- Allow cheese sauce to simmer, stirring often, for 5-6 minutes.

GIBLET GRAVY

2	**cups chicken broth**
1	**coarsely chopped hard-boiled egg**
¼	**cup coarsely chopped chicken or turkey giblets**
	cornstarch

- In a saucepan add all ingredients except cornstarch.
- Bring to a boil.
- Dissolve 1-2 teaspoons cornstarch in 1 tablespoon cold water.
- Gradually stir into gravy to desired thickness.

BOILED WATER

This receipe was provided by Jennifer who was a secretary at the Blue Willow Inn for two years. When Jennifer got married she could not boil water. While we were preparing the cookbook she advised us that this was the only thing she could cook other than peanut butter and jelly sandwiches. (We plan on giving Jennifer a complimentary copy of the cookbook.)

1 quart tap water

- Place water in saucepan.
- Turn burner to high.
- Cover water with lid.
- When steam appears coming out of top, water is boiling.

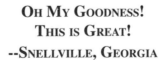

**OH MY GOODNESS!
THIS IS GREAT!
--SNELLVILLE, GEORGIA**

This is Susie, the Van Dykes' wonderful pet,
who is seen here posing with Olivia and Miss Billie.

EXPERIENCING
SOUPS, SALADS, ETC.

Once inside the Blue Willow Inn, *visitors are greeted by the warm smile of one of the friendly hostesses. Although reservations are not required, they are recommended. There is ample parking for buses and RVs.*

CHICKEN STEW

This recipe was given by Ann Lowe who is the head cook at the Blue Willow Inn Restaurant. Anytime Billie is not feeling well, Ann makes her chicken stew.

1	**broiler-fryer chicken**
1	**quart water**
1	**quart milk**
1	**cup butter**
2	**sleeves Saltine crackers**
	salt and pepper to taste

- Wash chicken thoroughly.
- Place 1 quart of water in stock pot. Add chicken and cook until tender.
- Remove chicken, reserving chicken broth.
- Add milk to broth and bring to a slow boil, stirring often to prevent scorching.
- Crush Saltine crackers and add to pot.
- Add salt and pepper.
- Allow to simmer, stirring often, until mixture thickens.
- Remove the skin and bones from chicken. Tear into bite size pieces.
- When pot thickens, add chicken.
- Add a little bit of love, the secret ingredient that makes you feel better.
- Serve hot.

CHICKEN AND DUMPLINGS, SERVED AS A SOUP BUT AS THICK AS STEW, IS SUPREMELY COMFORTING-- ALABASTER WHITE, SOFT, SMOOTH, AND AROMATIC. JANE AND MICHAEL STERN, *GOURMET*

CHICKEN AND DUMPLINGS

Chicken and Dumplings are served at almost every meal at the Blue Willow Inn Restaurant and has become a favorite of our guests. It takes a few minutes to prepare, but you can't beat this on a cold winter night. With crackers or toast this is a complete meal.

1	3-4 pound broiler-fryer chicken
2	quarts water
½	cup melted butter
2	teaspoons black pepper
1	teaspoon salt
2	cups self-rising flour
¼	cup shortening
¼	cup cold water

- In a stock pot combine water and chicken.
- Cook over medium-high heat until done (about one hour).
- Remove chicken from pot reserving chicken broth.
- Cool chicken in cold water. Remove bones, skin, and fat.
- Cut chicken into bite size pieces.
- In mixing bowl combine flour and salt.
- Cut in shortening until batter is coarse.
- Add water and mix well with your hands.
- Bring chicken broth back to a slow boil. Do not rapidly boil.
- With floured hands pinch quarter size pieces of flour and drop into chicken broth.
- Gently stir after adding several pinches.
- Repeat until you have used all the dumpling mix. Stir gently. (Cont.→)

- Add butter and black pepper. Stir gently.
- Allow to simmer 8-10 minutes.
- Slowly stir in chicken.
- Serve in soup bowls.

VEGETABLE SOUP

Vegetable soup can include such vegetables as snap beans, butter beans and lima beans. Leftover vegetables are good additions to vegetable soup. Cooked greens such as turnip greens, collards or cabbage are generally not used but can be included as a matter of personal choice.

4	**cups water**
½	**cup diced potatoes**
½	**cup sliced carrots**
½	**cup early June peas**
¼	**cup chopped celery**
¼	**cup sliced onions**
½	**cup fresh or frozen okra**
1	**cup mashed whole cooked tomatoes**
¾	**cup corn**
1	**pound cubed beef, optional for Vegetable-Beef soup**
1	**pound ham or hamhock, optional for Vegetable-Ham soup**
	salt and pepper to taste

- In stock pot combine all ingredients.
- Bring to a boil and allow to simmer for 1-2 hours until seasoned and done, stirring occasionally.

> **TO USE OUR FAMILY WORD--**
> **DELUMPTIOUS**
> **---NORCROSS, GEORGIA**

BRUNSWICK STEW

This is another recipe from Louis's dad. Louis fondly remembers each year his dad cooking his famous Brunswick Stew in a large black kettle in the back yard. He would start a couple of days ahead and prepare all of the vegetables fresh from the garden. When the annual Brunswick Stew Day arrived he would rise early and start the fire and begin cooking the stew. Louis has fond memories of watching him tend and care for his pot of Brunswick Stew all day long. When the stew was ready, family and neighbors would be waiting for their bowls. Late at night when the stew had cooled, it was poured into freezer bags and shared with everyone, but not all of the stew was given away. There was always extra stew in the freezer so that it could be enjoyed for several months. This recipe is a variation of the "original" recipe that took days of preparation and cooking, but there is no better stew ANYWHERE!

1	7-8 pound baking hen
4	pounds boneless stewing beef, cut into small pieces
4	pounds hamhocks
10	10-ounce can of shoepeg corn
	or equal amount of corn cut from cob
1	gallon whole, peeled tomatoes
4	pounds frozen baby lima beans
4	pounds frozen or fresh sweet peas
4	cups chopped onions
4	cups chopped celery
10	pounds potatoes, peeled and sliced
	BBQ Sauce (optional)
	Worcestershire Sauce (optional)
	salt and pepper to taste

In a 3 gallon stock pot, combine baking hen, stew beef and hamhocks. Cover with enough water to make 2¼ gallons. (Cont.→)

 Cook meats until fully done and remove all meat from pot.

Remove bones, fat and skin and chop meat into small pieces.

Skim fat from broth. Using a second 3 gallon stock pot, divide broth and meat equally between pots.

Divide all vegetables equally between the two pots. Do not use juice from canned tomatoes.

Cover pots to retain flavors and bring to a rapid boil, stirring often.

Boil rapidly for 8-10 minutes, stirring often to prevent sticking and burning.

Turn heat down and allow each pot to simmer for 3-4 hours.

Add salt and pepper as desired to season.

If desired, add sauces to flavor and season during cooking.

CLAM CHOWDER (QUICK & EASY)

This Clam Chowder recipe is from Louis's Aunt Dot.

1	**can Campbell's Clam Chowder**
1	**cup milk**
1	**tablespoon butter**
¼	**cup breaded clam pieces**
¼	**cup shredded Cheddar cheese**
	salt and pepper to taste

In heavy saucepan combine all ingredients.

Over medium heat bring to a slow boil, stirring often.

Turn heat down and simmer for 10-15 minutes, stirring often.

Yield: 4 servings

BLUEBERRY SALAD

This salad is always served on holidays and special family gatherings. It is our son, Chip's favorite dish at all special occasions. He enjoys it both as a salad and dessert.

1	8-ounce can crushed pineapple
1	6-ounce package blueberry Jello (blackberry can be substituted)
3	cups boiling water
1	16-ounce can blueberries, drained
1	8-ounce package sour cream
½	cup sugar
1	8-ounce package cream cheese, softened
½	cup chopped pecans

- Drain pineapple; reserve juice.
- Dissolve Jello in boiling water and stir in pineapple juice.
- Chill until consistency of unbeaten egg whites.
- Stir in pineapple and blueberries.
- Pour into two 10x6x1¾-inch pans and chill until firm.
- Combine sour cream, cheese and sugar. Mix until smooth or well blended.
- Spread over salad and top with pecans.

Yield: 8 servings.

NOTE: Several years ago Billie was preparing foods for a covered dish lunch at church--the blueberry salad and the vinegar base gelatin salad. Louis came into the kitchen and suggested that the Blueberry Salad topping would go well on the other congealed salad. Billie told Louis not to top the other salad with the blueberry salad topping, but as Billie was saying no, Louis was busily topping the

vinegar based gelatin salad anyway. Billie said nothing else. When they arrived at church for lunch, Billie placed her foods on the serving tables, and as usual, several of the church members headed straight for Billie's dishes. When Louis sat down to eat he had both the blueberry salad and the "other" salad that he had topped. When Louis ate the "other" salad, he could not swallow the Jello--the topping had reacted with the vinegar. Louis said that he was sure that "it had turned to poison." Billie made sure that everyone who had some of the "other salad" knew that this was Louis's salad and not hers. From that point forward, Louis has not acted like he knows more about cooking than Billie.

WATERGATE SALAD (GREEN STUFF)

This recipe was given to us by Kim Unruh who worked for the Van Dykes for several years. She worked as our salad and dessert person. She often made her favorite salad she called "Green Stuff."

1	**3-ounce package instant pistachio pudding**
1	**cup miniature marshmallows**
1	**14-ounce can crushed pineapple**
1	**9-ounce package Cool Whip**
⅓	**cup chopped pecans**

- Mix all ingredients.
- Whip until fluffy.
- Refrigerate and serve cold.

ALMOND AND ORANGE SALAD

This recipe was submitted by Mildred Tribble who lives in Social Circle.
This goes good with special dinners or luncheons.

2	sliced garden onions
½	head chopped endive, if desired
1	can number 3 mandarin orange sections
2	tablespoons chopped fresh parsley
½	cup carmelized almonds

 Mix above ingredients and carmelized almonds together.

 Pour dressing over immediately before serving.

CARMELIZED ALMONDS

Use in Almond and Orange Salad.

½	cup almonds, sliced
4	tablespoons sugar

 Mix sugar and almonds in heavy pan on high heat.

 Stir for 3 minutes.

 Spread apart.

ALMOND AND ORANGE SALAD DRESSING

¼	cup salad oil
2	tablespoons vinegar
2	tablespoons sugar
5	drops Tabasco sauce
½	teaspoon salt

 Shake all ingredients together.

Hot Chicken Salad

This recipe was given to us by Scottie Sherrill whose husband, Frank has been mayor of Social Circle for several years. Scottie has become a good friend and customer of the Blue Willow Inn Restaurant.

2	**cups chopped, cooked boneless chicken**
2	**cups chopped celery**
½	**cup mayonnaise**
½	**teaspoon salt**
2	**tablespoons grated onions**
½	**can condensed cream of mushroom soup**
½	**cup chopped green bell peppers**
2	**tablespoons lemon juice**
3	**tablespoons chopped pimentos**
1	**teaspoon Worcestershire sauce**

Mix all ingredients. Pour into a baking dish and top with the following ingredients:

¾	**cup grated Cheddar cheese**
½	**cup slivered almonds**
2	**cups crushed potato chips**

Bake for 30 minutes at 350 degrees.

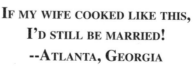

IF MY WIFE COOKED LIKE THIS,
I'D STILL BE MARRIED!
--ATLANTA, GEORGIA

HORSERADISH SALAD

Good with Roast Beef or other beef dishes. This was given to us by Francis Jones to use at a Chamber of Commerce function we catered for them. We served a steamboat round.

1	3-ounce package lime flavored gelatin
1	3-ounce package lemon flavored gelatin
2	cups boiling water
1	20-ounce can crushed pineapple, drained and chilled
1	12-ounce package cottage cheese
1	cup mayonnaise
1	cup finely chopped pecans
4	tablespoons horseradish
3	tablespoons lemon juice
¼	teaspoon salt
1	14-ounce can sweetened condensed milk

TOPPING

½	cup mayonnaise
½	cup sour cream
1	teaspoon horseradish

- Dissolve gelatin in boiling water and cool.
- Add pineapple.
- In separate bowl combine cottage cheese with mayonnaise.
- Mix until smooth. Add to gelatin mix.
- Add all other ingredients and stir until mixture begins to congeal.
- Pour into mold or 13x9x2-inch pan and refrigerate overnight.
- For topping, combine all ingredients and mix well.
- Serve gelatin on bed of lettuce with topping spooned on top.

81

Cottage Cheese Salad

1	12-ounce package cottage cheese
1	10-ounce can mandarin orange sections, drained
½	cup chopped nuts
1	small container Cool Whip
1	20-ounce can crushed pineapple
1	3-ounce package orange Jello

- Combine cottage cheese and Cool Whip and blend gently.
- Add fruit and nuts and mix gently.
- Add dry Jello and mix.
- Chill.

Yield: 6-8 servings

Louis's Potato Salad

6	medium all-purpose potatoes
4	hard-boiled eggs
¼	cup chopped green salad olives
¼	cup mayonnaise
1	tablespoon prepared mustard
	salt and pepper to taste
	paprika, optional
	parsley, optional

- Peel and cut potatoes into ½-inch cubes.
- Cover with water in a stock pot and bring to a boil.
- Cook until potatoes are just beginning to test tender

with a fork.
- Remove from heat and cool in cold water to stop cooking process.
- Slice the eggs into small slices.
- In a mixing bowl, add all ingredients except one egg, paprika and parsley.
- Mix gently and transfer potato salad to the serving bowl.
- Layer remaining egg on top.
- If desired, garnish with a small amount of paprika and fresh parsley sprigs.
- Cover and refrigerate until serving.

POTATO SALAD

6	**medium all-purpose potatoes**
4	**hard-boiled eggs**
¼	**cup sweet picklc relish**
½	**cup finely chopped onions, optional**
¼	**cup mayonnaise**
1	**tablespoon prepared mustard**
¼	**cup chopped green salad olives, optional**
	salt and black pepper to taste
	paprika, optional
	parsley, optional

- Peel and chop potatoes into 1-inch cubes.
- Cover with water in a stock pot and bring to a boil.
- Cook until potatoes are just beginning to test tender.
- Remove from heat and cool in cold water to stop cooking process. (Cont.→)

 Slice the eggs into small slices.

 In a mixing bowl, add all ingredients except one egg, paprika and parsley.

 Mix gently and transfer potato salad to serving bowl.

 Layer remaining egg on top. If desired, garnish with small amount of paprika and fresh parsley sprigs.

 Cover and refrigerate until serving.

COLE SLAW

1	**medium head of cabbage**
¼	**cup shredded purple cabbage, optional**
1	**heaping tablespoon of sweet pickle relish**
2	**carrots, shredded**
¼	**cup mayonnaise**
1	**tablespoon granulated sugar**
1	**tablespoon white vinegar (optional)**
	salt and black pepper to taste

 In a mixing bowl, combine all ingredients.

 Stir to mix well.

VARIATION: APPLE COLE SLAW

 Delete pickle relish and vinegar.

 Cut 1 or 2 Granny Smith or Rome apples into small cubes. Do not peel.

 Combine with slaw and mix.

 This adds a whole new flavor to cole slaw.

Yield: 4-6 servings

> **BRILLIANT FOOD!**
> ---**LONDON, ENGLAND**

Marinated Vegetable Salad

¼   **cup black olives**
¼   **cup green olives**
2-3   **sliced radishes**
1   **bottle Italian salad dressing**
2-3   **cups broccoli florets**
2-3   **cups cauliflower florets**
1   **cups sliced squash**
1   **cups sliced cucumber**
1   **pt. cherry tomatoes**

- Prepare four cups of the desired combination of broccoli, cauliflower, squash, cucumber and cherry tomatoes.
- Combine with olives and radishes.
- Pour Italian dressing over vegetables.
- Marinate refrigerated overnight.

Kraut Salad

1   **pint chopped and drained sauerkraut**
1   **cup chopped onions**
1   **cup chopped celery**
1   **chopped green bell pepper**
1   **cup granulated sugar**
½   **cup vinegar**
½   **cup salad oil**

- Mix all ingredients well.
- Let stand for two hours. (Cont.→)

 Best if prepared the day before and refrigerated overnight.

 Store in a sealed container.

Buttermilk Congealed Salad

This recipe was submitted by Mae Morrow, the manager of the Blue Willow Inn Restaurant. She came to work for Louis and Billie in 1988 when they opened their restaurant at the American Legion facility in Monroe, Georgia. Mae has been a valuable asset to both the Blue Willow Inn and the Van Dykes since joining their staff. Without Mae, the Blue Willow Inn would not be the same. She first served her Buttermilk Congealed Salad shortly after joining the staff in Monroe, and it has for several years been a favorite of customers and is always served on special occasions. Mae usually prepares the salad herself to assure consistency and quality.

1	**3-ounce package orange Jello**
1	**8-ounce can crushed pineapple**
2	**cups buttermilk**
1	**6-ounce package of Cool Whip**
2	**cups chopped pecans**

 Drain juice from pineapple into a small saucepan.

 Add Jello and cook over low heat until Jello dissolves.

 Cool.

 Mix buttermilk and Cool Whip.

 Add pecans and Jello to mixture.

 Pour into a mold or casserole dish and refrigerate.

 Serve when firm.

Yield: 6 servings

CARROT-RAISIN SALAD
This is a good dish for luncheons.

8-10   large carrots, shredded
½   cup raisins
½   cup chopped pineapple
¼   cup mayonnaise
1   teaspoon granulated sugar

 In mixing bowl, combine all ingredients.

 Stir to mix well.

WALDORF SALAD

2   cups diced apples
¾   cup chopped celery
¾   cup coarsely chopped pecans
⅔   cup raisins
2   bananas, sliced
¼-⅓   cup mayonnaise

 When selecting apples select hard, tart apples.

 Wash apples and leave the peeling on.

 If apples and sliced bananas are not placed in salad immediately, toss in ¼ cup water with 2 teaspoons of lemon juice.

 Mix all ingredients.

 Chill.

Yield: 8 servings

87

Bing Frozen Cherry Salad

This recipe was submitted by Sandi McClain, manager of
The Blue Willow Gift Shop.

1	8-ounce package cream cheese
1	8-ounce package sour cream
½	cup sugar
1	cup chopped pecans
1	16-ounce can crushed pineapple
1	16-ounce can dark pitted cherries, in own juice, drained
1½	cups minimarshmallows
1-2	drops red food coloring

- Mix all ingredients except the fruit in food processor.
- After mixing, pour into a mixing bowl and stir in pine apple and cherries.
- Pour into a 13x9x2 inch casserole dish and freeze.
- Cut into squares.

Hamburger

1	pound lean ground beef
1	juicy, ripe tomato
4	slices American cheese, if desired
8	slices cooked bacon, if desired
4	slices sweet or mild yellow onion, if desired
4	hamburger buns
	iceberg, leaf lettuce
	sliced hamburger dill pickles, if desired
	mayonnaise, ketchup, mustard
	salt and black pepper to taste

- Divide ground beef into four equal sections.
- Pat out each section into a patty. Add salt and pepper if desired.
- Cook in large skillet over medium heat, on a charcoal grill or in the oven at 350 degrees.
- If cooking on a grill or in a skillet, turn meat a couple of times.
- Cook until center is done, but do not overcook.
- Cooked hamburger should be juicy.
- If cheese is desired, melt cheese during the final minutes of cooking.
- If using a grill or oven the inside of the buns can be toasted, if desired.
- Spread mayonnaise on the inside of the buns both on top and bottom.
- Spread ketchup on bottom of bun.
- Place hamburger on ketchup side.
- Spread mustard on top of the bun on top of the mayonnaise.
- Place lettuce on top of the hamburger patty.
- Next place tomato and onion.
- Last is the pickles.
- Close the bun.

NOTE: It is important to arrange the ingredients in the proper order for the proper blending of tastes.

Yield: 4 hamburgers

A NICE RESPITE!
--CHAPPAGUA, NEW YORK

HOT DOGS

This is an all-American treat that is great for snacks or meals.

desired number of all-beef hot dogs
sliced American cheese, if desired
hot dog chili, if desired
sauerkraut, if desired
coleslaw, if desired
sweet pickle relish, if desired
ketchup and mustard, if desired

- There are several methods of cooking hot dogs.
- Put enough water in small saucepan to cover hot dogs and bring to boil.
- Place hot dogs in boiling water and allow to boil 3-4 minutes.
- Hot dogs can be cooked in a microwave oven using medium heat for 20-40 seconds depending on the wattage of the microwave oven.
- Hot dogs can be grilled on a charcoal grill. When grilling turn the hot dogs often to prevent burning.
- When using cheese on a hot dog the hot dogs should be partially split open with a knife and the cavity filled with cheese.
- All of the above ingredients can be used on hot dogs.
- If using sauerkraut do not use slaw.

SOUTHERN HOSPITALITY IS GREAT!
---LAMBACH, AUSTRIA

HAM & CHEESE SANDWICH

Louis makes one of the best ham and cheese sandwiches to be found. The ingredients are not different than most ham and cheese sandwiches. The important part is how the sandwich is layered to excite the taste buds. If it is just thrown together, it will not be the same.

**sandwich bread
sliced ham
American cheese (Kraft Deluxe sliced American
cheese is best, but if preferred, use Swiss)
iceberg lettuce
juicy, big ripe red tomato
Kraft Miracle Whip salad dressing or mayonnaise
prepared mustard
salt and black pepper**

- Spread mayonnaise on each piece of white or whole wheat sliced bread.
- Place the ham on the mayonnaise side of one piece of bread.
- Follow with the cheese.
- Next add desired amount of lettuce (iceberg lettuce is the only right lettuce to use on this sandwich).
- Place one to two slices of tomato on top of the lettuce.
- Spread mustard on top of the mayonnaise on remaining piece of bread.
- Salt and pepper to taste the tomato.
- Serve with potato chips and enjoy. You better make two sandwiches because you will not be able to stop with just one.

GRILLED CHEESE SANDWICH

Grilled cheese sandwiches have always been an American favorite. Louis and Billie enjoy grilled cheese sandwiches on cold winter nights with tomato soup.

**sliced sandwich bread
American cheese (Kraft Deluxe sliced cheese
is the best)
mayonnaise
butter or margarine
sliced ham (optional)**

- Spread a small amount of mayonnaise on each piece of bread.
- Place 1-2 slices of American cheese on half of the bread on the mayonnaise side. Close each sandwich.
- Butter the outside of each sandwich on both sides with a small amount of butter.
- Place into a frying pan over medium heat. Brown both sides of the sandwich, turning once.
- For grilled ham and cheese, add ham to the sandwich at the same time as the cheese.
- For even better grilled ham and cheese, grill the sliced ham first in the skillet.

CLUB SANDWICH

**toasted white bread
cooked bacon
cooked ham, thinly sliced
cooked chicken or turkey, thinly sliced**

sliced American cheese
sliced Swiss cheese
mayonnaise
mustard, if desired
juicy tomato, sliced
iceberg, leaf lettuce

- Use three slices of toasted white bread for each club sandwich.
- On the bottom slice spread mayonnaise.
- Next place the sliced ham, then sliced turkey or chicken.
- Place the Swiss cheese on top of the turkey.
- Spread mayonnaise on both sides of the next piece of toasted bread.
- Place the slice of bread on top of the turkey.
- Place two slices of bacon on the bread.
- Place the American cheese next.
- Then place lettuce followed by tomato.
- Spread mayonnaise on one side of the remaining piece of toasted bread.
- Add mustard if desired.
- Cut sandwich into quarters, cutting diagonally across the bread.
- Place a long toothpick in the center of each sandwich to keep the sections together.
- Serve with potato chips and a pickle spear.
  TIP: Grill the ham first and add one extra piece of American cheese to melt on ham while grilling.

Sweetened Iced Tea

The South is famous for sweetened iced tea. Most Southerners drink their tea too sweet and too strong according to our "Yankee" friends. At the Blue WIllow Inn we serve our tea a "little too sweet" and strong. For those who like sweetened iced tea but not too sweet we mix with unsweetened tea (the kind Northerners drink). Sweetened iced tea is the beverage of choice for Southerners at lunch and supper and as refreshment during the day, hence the nickname "the Champagne of the South."

1	**gallon water**
4-5	**family sized tea bags**
3	**cups sugar**
	lemon slices to garnish, optional
	sprig of mint

- Bring water to a boil in a 1½ gallon saucepan.
- Turn off heat and add tea bags.
- Cover to steep 10-15 minutes. For stronger tea allow to sit longer.
- Add desired amount of sugar and stir to dissolve.
- Allow to cool and pour over glass of ice.
- Garnish with lemon and mint.

Veranda Tea Punch

1	**quart Gingerale or Coca-Cola**
1	**quart soda water**
2	**cups tea infusion**
⅔	**cup sugar**
⅔	**cup water**

juice of 4 oranges

- Combine ⅔ cup of sugar and ⅔ cup water to make sugar syrup.
- Boil together for 10 minutes.
- Mix orange juice and sugar syrup.
- Add hot tea and let cool.
- When ready to serve, add Coca-Cola or Gingerale and soda water.
- Garnish with lemon and orange slices.
  Yield: 20 servings

LEMONADE

Lemonade is served daily at the Blue Willow Inn Restaurant. While our guests are waiting to be seated, our ladies dressed in antebellum gowns serve lemonade on the porches and grounds. This lemonade is refreshing anytime.

**3   or more fresh lemons
Country Time lemonade mix
sugar**

- A shortcut to lemonade is to use Country Time Lemonade Mix as a base for lemonade.
- Follow the directions on the carton for desired amount of lemonade.
- For each 8 ounces of lemonade, use 2 teaspoons of sugar and 1 fresh-squeezed lemon.
- Squeeze the lemon in a bowl and remove seeds.
- Pour the lemon juice and pulp into the mix and stir.
  (Cont.→)

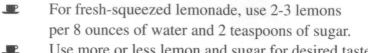 For fresh-squeezed lemonade, use 2-3 lemons per 8 ounces of water and 2 teaspoons of sugar.

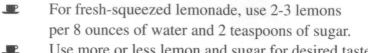 Use more or less lemon and sugar for desired taste.

CHATHAM ARTILLERY PUNCH

This recipe has been handed down for years in Savannah, home of the Chatham Artillery. The punch, and it does carry a "punch," is often served for large gatherings in Savannah.

1½	**gallons Catawba wine**
½	**gallon rum**
1	**quart gin**
1	**quart brandy**
½	**pint Benedictine**
2	**quarts maraschino cherries**
1½	**quarts rye whiskey**
1½	**gallons strong tea**
2	**pounds brown sugar**
1½	**quarts orange juice**
1½	**quarts lemon juice**
1	**case Champagne**

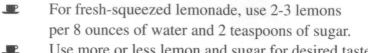 Mix all ingredients except champagne.

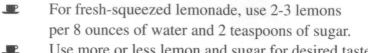 Mix 36-48 hours prior to serving.

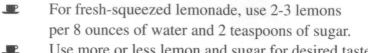 Add one case of champagne when ready to serve.
Yield: A LOT!

WE HEARD ABOUT YOU IN SWITZERLAND!
---**BOSTON, MASSACHUSETTS**

The Lewis Grizzard Room *is one of the dining areas at the Blue Willow Inn. The room was named in honor of the famous author and columnist whose article about the restaurant was the miracle the Van Dykes had prayed for. On display in the Grizzard room are several of the humorist's books and memorabilia.*

The Savannah Room *features a warm fireplace which beautifully complements the Inn's decor of deep greens and burgundies. Note the blue willow china on the tables--it's not just for decoration at the Blue Willow Inn!*

The Blue Room
is one of the smalle
rooms on the second
floor which is open to
guests and smal
parties.

**The Grand
Hallway** *on the
second floor over-
looks the beautiful
stairway.*

The Walton Room, *which houses the buffet service area, is the largest room on the main level. Guests choose from a delectable selection of four to five meats, nine to ten Southern style vegetables, soup, chicken and dumplings, salad fixings as well as homemade biscuits, muffins and cornbread. Last but not least is a delicious spread of pies, cobblers, puddings and cake.*

The Garden Room *was formerly part of the back porch.*

The pool and poolhouse formerly used by the community as recreational facilities in the 1950s have been converted into a Gift Shop and fountain area. Guests to the Blue Willow Inn can browse in the shop for Southern collectibles and keepsakes or enjoy the relaxing fountains and gardens.

(L) Sandi McClain, manager of the Blue Willow Inn Gift Shop and interior decorator of Magnolia Hall.

Ann Lowe, *the head cook at The Blue Willow Inn, helps create the award winning Southern dishes that approximately 5,000 guests enjoy weekly. Here Ann diplays the dish dubbed "to-die-for fried chicken."*

The Savannah Room *in its Christmas finest.*

The Van Dykes were serving Fried Green Tomatoes long before the movie came out.

Ludlow Porch has said of the Van Dykes, "No vegetable on the planet is safe from their wonderful magic."

With delicious soups like this vegetable soup pictured here and chicken and dumplings, not to mention all of the other choices on the buffet at Blue Willow Inn, customers can frequently be overheard commenting, "My diet starts tomorrow!"

If visitors time their visits to the Inn just right, they may find Louis's baby back ribs on the buffet. The ribs are coated in Louis's special sauce, of which he will reveal only one secret ingredient--Coca-Cola.

Magnolia Hall is one of the beautiful old homes built in Social Circle in the early 1900s. In 1995, Louis and Billie Van Dyke purchased the old home and renovated it to accomodate large groups and parties. Magnolia Hall is now open as a catering and special events facility.

Social Circle boasts many charming and historical homes such as the one pictured at left.

EXPERIENCING
FRUITS AND VEGETABLES

The grounds of the Blue Willow Inn Restaurant *feature seasonal vegetation and provide a scenic route through which visitors may wander and enjoy the Blue Willow experience a few minutes longer.*

COLLARD GREENS

Collard Greens are God's gift to the South!

1	bunch fresh collard greens
1	ounce bacon grease
½	teaspoon salt
1	tablespoon granulated sugar
6	ounces fatback or hamhock
¼	teaspoon black pepper
¼	teaspoon baking soda
1	quart water

- Pull the leaves of collards from stems. Discard stems. (Small stems may be left in with leaves.)
- Coarsely chop or tear collards.
- Wash thoroughly in cold water and drain.
- Add all ingredients.
- Bring to a boil and cook at slow boil for 2 hours or until tender.

TURNIP GREENS

Serve with hot pepper sauce or tomato chutney.

1	large bunch of fresh (or frozen) turnip greens
2-3	quarts of water
2	ounces bacon grease
6	ounces fatback or ham
½	teaspoon salt
½	teaspoon sugar, optional
	pepper to taste

- Separate stems from leaves and throw away stems. Wash leaves in cold water.
- In stock pot, combine all other ingredients.
- Bring to a boil and add turnip greens. Boil over medium heat 1½ hours until tender.
- If desired, wash and dice turnips and add to boiling water and cook with turnip greens.

Rutabagas

3-4	**rutabagas**
3-4	**cups water**
¼	**cup butter**
	salt and pepper to taste

- Peel and dice rutabagas into bite size pieces.
- Place in a stock pot.
- Cover with water and add other ingredients.
- Bring to a boil and cook for 1 to 1½ hours until tender.

Twice Baked Potatoes

When Louis and Billie first moved to Social Circle in 1970, their next door neighbors and old friends, Bill and Sophia DeMoss, invited them over for dinner. Twice baked potatoes were on the menu. Louis and Billie have cooked and served them in their restaurants since 1985. When they are served at the Blue Willow, the kitchen struggles to keep up with the demand.

4	**baking potatoes**
⅓	**stick butter (Cont.→)**

½ cup grated Cheddar cheese, divided
¼ cup sour cream
   scant ¼ cup milk
   salt and pepper to taste

- Bake potatoes in skins until tender. Cool for 20 minutes or until cool enough to handle.
- Cut in halves lengthwise and scoop out potatoes into bowl.
- Mash with fork. Add sour cream, half of cheese, butter and a little milk
- Mix well.
- Season to taste.
- Scoop potatoes back into skins and place on cookie sheet. Top with remaining grated cheese.
- Bake at 350 degrees until cheese melts (12-15 minutes).
- Serve hot.

Yield: 8 servings.

CREAMED POTATOES OR MASHED POTATOES

6   medium potatoes
¼   cup milk
⅓   cup melted butter
1   tablespoon mayonnaise, optional
1½ quarts water
    salt and pepper to taste

- Peel and dice potatoes.
- In a saucepan bring water to a boil.
- Add salt, pepper and potatoes.
- Boil until tender, about 15-20 minutes.

 Pour off water and add milk and butter.

 With a potato masher or hand-held electric mixer, cream the potatoes.

 If the potatoes are too stiff, add a little more milk and butter.

Yield: 4-6 servings.

SCALLOPED POTATOES

3-4   medium potatoes
½   cup butter, divided
2   tablespoons flour
1   cup milk
1   small onion, sliced
      salt and pepper to taste

 Wash, peel and slice potatoes into ¼-inch rounds.

 Cover with water in a stock pot and cook just until tender. Do not overcook.

 In a small saucepan combine ¼ cup butter, flour and milk.

 Cook over medium heat until mixture begins to thicken.

 Saute onion in butter. Add to milk mixture.

 Add salt and pepper.

 Place potatoes in casserole dish and pour mixture over potatoes.

 Cook uncovered at 350 degrees for 25-30 minutes.

NOTE: For scalloped potatoes au gratin, add 2 table-spoons of Cheese Whiz and ½ cup grated Cheddar cheese to saucepan with milk mixture.

101

Roasted New Potatoes

8   small new red potatoes
¼   cup butter
½   teaspoon garlic salt
¼   cup chopped parsley
       salt and pepper to taste

- Wash potatoes.
- Cut in half and place on ungreased baking sheet.
- Brush each potato with butter and sprinkle remaining in gredients on top of each potato.
- Cook uncovered for 20-25 minutes at 350 degrees until potatoes begin to turn light brown.

Potato Cakes

4   cups leftover mashed potatoes
1   cup flour
6   eggs
¼   cup chopped onions
3   tablespoons bacon grease
       cooking oil

- Saute onions in bacon grease. Chopped bacon can be added if desired.
- In a mixing bowl combine all ingredients and mix well. Do not beat.
- Pour enough cooking oil into a heavy skillet to cover bottom.
- Form mixture into patties ¾-inch thick and 2½-3 inches

in diameter.

 Place in hot oil and cook each side until golden brown.

 Add small amounts of oil as needed.

NEW RED POTATOES

2	**pounds small new red potatoes**
½	**cup butter, divided**
½	**teaspoon salt**
	chopped parsley

 Wash potatoes.

 Place in stock pot and add enough water to cover plus one cup.

 Add half the butter and salt.

 Bring to a boil and allow to boil for 16-18 minutes until tested done with a fork.

 Remove potatoes from water and place in serving bowl.

 Pour remaining butter over potatoes and sprinkle with chopped parsley.

Yield: 4-6 servings.

FRIED ONION RINGS

Good by themselves or as a topping on green bean casserole.
They also complement steaks.

1	**large onion, sliced**
1	**cup buttermilk**
2	**eggs, beaten**
2	**cups self-rising flour**

vegetable oil
salt and pepper to taste

- In a mixing bowl combine buttermilk, eggs, salt, pepper and 1 tablespoon of flour. Mix well.
- Preheat vegetable oil in large deep frying pan to 325 degrees.
- Place onion rings in buttermilk/egg mixture.
- Dredge in flour.
- Place in frying pan and cook 8-10 minutes until golden brown, turning twice.
- Drain on paper towel.

BAKED VIDALIA ONIONS

*Vidalia onions are the best, but if they are not available,
Texas sweets or Washington State sweets are good.*

6	medium Vidalia onions
½	cup butter
½	cup shredded Cheddar cheese
½	cup crushed croutons
¼	cup water
	salt and pepper to taste

- Peel onions.
- Make two cuts diagonally across each onion cutting ½ to ⅔ through the onion.
- Sprinkle with croutons, salt and pepper.
- Pour a small amount of butter over each onion using all of the butter.
- Bake uncovered 25-30 minutes at 350 degrees or in the microwave for 12-15 minutes until tender. (Cont.→)

Remove from oven and top with Cheddar cheese.

Return to oven to melt cheese.

Yield: 6 servings.

Fried Green Tomatoes

The Blue Willow Inn's fried green tomatoes have played a big role in making the restaurant famous. In March of 1992 (shortly after the restaurant opened), columnist Lewis Grizzard came to the Blue Willow Inn to dine. On the buffet we were serving fried green tomatoes. We usually served them only once every week to ten days. After leaving, Mr. Grizzard wrote a column about the Blue Willow Inn Restaurant and our food with emphasis on the fried green tomatoes. The column appeared in approximately 280 newspapers nationwide. This one event took the Blue Willow Inn from a new, struggling establishment to a successful restaurant in one weekend. The column is reprinted in full at the beginning of this book. We now serve fried green tomatoes at every meal.

3	**green tomatoes**
2	**cups vegetable oil**
1½	**cups self-rising flour**
1	**teaspoon salt**
1	**teaspoon black pepper**
1½	**cups buttermilk**
2	**eggs**

Wash and slice tomatoes (approximately ¼-inch slices).

Mix buttermilk and eggs in a mixing bowl.

Add ½ the salt and pepper and 1 tablespoon of flour.

Mix well.

Place tomato slices in the buttermilk/egg mix.

Preheat the oil to 350 degrees in a heavy skillet or electric fryer. (Cont.→)

- Mix the remaining flour, salt and pepper in a mixing bowl.
- Toss the tomato slices in the flour.
- Place in the oil and fry until golden brown, turning two to three times.
- Cook until crisp and drain on paper towels.
- Serve immediately.

  NOTE: Tomato chutney is a good complement to this dish.

STEWED TOMATOES

Louis's mother used to serve stewed tomatoes with creamed potatoes and fried fish.

1	**16-ounce can whole tomatoes**
2	**slices bacon, cooked and chopped**
1	**tablespoon bacon grease**
3-4	**slices white bread**
¼	**teaspoon sugar, optional**
	salt and pepper to taste

- Pour tomatoes with juice into small pot.
- Mash tomatoes with fork.
- Add bacon grease, bacon, salt, pepper and sugar.
- Bring to a boil.
- Tear bread into strips. Add to tomatoes and stir.
- Remove from heat and serve over rice or creamed potatoes.

> **LONG DRIVE, BUT IT WAS WORTH IT!**
> **---HALIFAX, NOVA SCOTIA, CANADA**

OKRA AND TOMATOES
Good over rice.

2   slices bacon, fried crisp (reserve bacon grease)
1   medium onion, chopped
1   16-ounce can whole tomatoes
1   10-ounce package fresh or frozen okra
     salt and pepper to taste

 In a heavy skillet saute onion in bacon grease.
 Add okra and tomatoes.
 Crumble bacon and add.
 Season with salt and pepper.
 With spoon, cut tomatoes in quarters.
 Cook for 15-20 minutes until done.

FRIED OKRA

2   pounds fresh okra
2½   cups water
1   cup plain cornmeal
1   cup all-purpose flour
2   cups vegetable oil
      salt and pepper to taste

 Wash and cut okra discarding the ends.
 Pour water in mixing bowl.
 Pour cooking oil in large heavy skillet and preheat oil.
 Place cut okra in water to moisten.
 Mix flour, cornmeal, salt and pepper. (Cont.➡)

- Remove okra from water and toss in flour mixture.
- Place each piece separately in heated oil.
- Cook until golden brown, gently stirring after butter has begun to set.
- Drain on paper towel.

BOILED OKRA

1	**pound fresh okra, stemmed**
	OR
1	**package frozen okra**
2	**cups water**
	salt and pepper to taste

- Cover okra in stock pot with water.
- Season to taste with salt and pepper.
- Simmer over medium heat 18-20 minutes until tender.

SKILLET SQUASH

8	**yellow squash**
1	**cup water**
¾	**cup melted butter, divided**
2	**ounces bacon grease**
1	**small, thinly sliced onion**
4	**slices bacon, fried crisp and chopped**
	salt and pepper to taste

- Wash and slice squash.
- In large skillet, cook 1 cup water, ½ cup butter, bacon

grease and onion until onion is tender.

- Add squash, bacon and seasonings.
- Cook until desired tenderness.
- Drain.
- Pour remaining butter over squash and serve.
  Yield: 6 servings

FRIED SQUASH

6	**yellow gooseneck or zucchini squash**
2	**cups water**
1	**cup buttermilk**
½	**teaspoon salt**
1½	**cups self-rising flour, divided**
1	**egg, beaten**
2	**cups vegetable oil**
	dash pepper

- Wash and slice squash. Discard ends.
- Place water in a mixing bowl and place sliced squash in water.
- Heat oil in large, heavy skillet.
- In a mixing bowl combine buttermilk, salt, pepper, egg and 1 tablespoon of flour and mix well.
- Remove squash from water and place in buttermilk mixture.
- Toss squash in remaining flour, coating each piece well.
- Place each piece in oil. When batter begins to set, stir gently.
- Cook until golden brown. Drain on paper towel.

Acorn Squash

2   **acorn squash**
⅔   **cup cracker crumbs**
½   **cup melted butter**
3   **teaspoons light brown sugar**
½   **teaspoon salt**
¼   **teaspoon nutmeg**

- Cut the squash in half and remove seeds.
- Mix all other ingredients together.
- Spoon equal amounts into each squash half.
- Bake at 350 degrees for 50-60 minutes until tender and brown.
  Yield: 4 servings.

Stuffed Zucchini Squash

2   **large (10-inch) zucchini squash**
6   **yellow gooseneck squash**
¼   **cup chopped onions**
2   **tablespoons melted butter**
4   **slices bacon, cooked crisp**
1   **cup grated Cheddar cheese, divided**
1   **ounce bacon grease**
1   **cup Ritz cracker crumbs, divided**
¼   **teaspoon salt**
    pepper to taste

- Wash and slice yellow squash, discarding ends.
- Place sliced yellow squash in saucepan and cover with water.

- Bring to a boil and cook until tender, 4-5 minutes.
- Wash zucchini squash and cut in half lengthwise.
- Using a knife or spoon hull out the center of the zucchini squash from end to end, making sure to leave the ends intact.
- In small skillet heat bacon grease and butter.
- Saute onions in skillet until tender.
- In mixing bowl combine meat from zucchini squash, cooked yellow squash (drained), bacon, ¾ cup cracker crumbs, ¾ cup cheese and onions. Mix but do not beat.
- Spoon mixture into the hulls of the zucchini squash.
- Place in casserole dish with ¼ inch of water and bake uncovered at 350 degrees for 40-50 minutes until done.
- Top with remaining cracker crumbs and cheese. Return to oven to melt cheese.
- Cut each stuffed zucchini into three sections.
  Yield: 6 servings.

BLACK-EYED PEAS

1	**gallon water**
½	**cup dry black-eyed peas**
2	**tablespoons bacon grease**
4	**ounces fatback**
4	**ounces hamhock or ham**
	salt and pepper to taste

- In a large pan cover black-eyed peas with water.
- Rinse well and drain. Rinse again and discard peas that float to the top. (Cont.fi)

- In a large stock pot, combine 1 gallon of water and black-eyed peas.
- Add all other ingredients.
- Bring to a boil then turn down to simmer for 1 hour. Stir often while simmering.

  NOTE: These will stick and scorch if the water is allowed to cook down too low. If more water is needed during cooking, add water.

  Yield: 6-8 servings.

CREAMED PEAS

1	**16-ounce can LeSeur brand early June peas**
½	**cup milk**
2	**tablespoons flour**
2	**tablespoons melted butter**
	salt and pepper to taste

- Combine the butter and flour in a saucepan.
- Pour half the juice from the peas and the milk into the saucepan.
- Over medium heat bring to a slow boil being careful not to scorch the milk.
- Simmer until liquid is the consistency of gravy.
- Add peas and seasoning.
- Simmer for 5-8 minutes.

> **DIET STARTS TOMORROW!**
> **---EATONTON, GEORGIA**

GREEN BEANS

1⅔	cups water
1	28-ounce can Italian cut green beans
4	ounces fatback
4	ounces cooked ham or hamhock
2	tablespoons bacon grease
¼	teaspoon brown sugar
	salt and pepper to taste

 In a stock pot combine all ingredients except green beans. Bring to a boil.

 Drain juice off green beans and add to boiling stock pot.

 Bring back to a boil and allow to slow boil for 20-25 minutes to season.

Yield: 4-6 servings.

GREEN BEANS IN BLANKETS

Another dish introduced to Louis and Billie by Sophia DeMoss, their next door neighbor in Social Circle. This dish is great as a vegetable dish with a meal or as an appetizer with finger foods.

1	16-ounce can whole green beans
1	pound bacon
1	bottle Catalina salad dressing

 Drain liquid from beans.

 Cut bacon in halves and wrap 4-5 beans in 1 piece of bacon. Continue until all beans and bacon are gone.

 Place cut side of bacon down in Pyrex baking dish.

 Pour Catalina dressing over beans. (Cont.→)

113

-  Bake at 350 degrees for 45 minutes or until bacon is done.
-  Drain grease from dish and serve in same dish or transfer to another dish.

Yield: 4 servings

BAKED BEANS

These hearty baked beans are a real treat when served with BBQ or hamburgers. They're a real crowd pleaser.

1	**pound ground beef**
1	**pound mild sausage links, cut into pieces**
1	**large chopped onion**
1	**large chopped green bell pepper**
4	**tablespoons ketchup**
¼	**cup granulated sugar**
4	**teaspoons mustard**
¼	**cup molasses**
¼	**cup brown sugar**
2	**28-ounce cans pork and beans**
1	**14-ounce can dark red kidney beans**
1	**14-ounce can light red kidney beans**
1-2	**teaspoons French's Chilli-O mix (to taste)**

-  Brown ground beef over medium heat in a large skillet.
-  When beef begins to come apart and is partially brown, add onion, bell pepper and sausage.
-  Cook until brown and pour off excess grease.
-  Turn heat down and add chili mix and stir well.
-  Add ketchup, sugar, mustard, molasses, brown sugar and juice from beans.
-  Mix well and cook for 2-3 minutes, stirring often.
-  Add beans and turn heat to high until bubbly, stirring often

or beans will stick.

 Turn heat down to simmer for 45 minutes or pour into a baking dish and bake for 45 minutes at 350 degrees.

NOTE: Mixture can be topped with strips of bacon prior to baking.

CORN

There are several types of corn available. The quickest is canned corn. The best is fresh corn cut off the ears. Frozen corn can be almost as good as fresh corn if you purchase the best quality available. Corn on the cob can be either fresh or frozen. The varieties of corn most often used are whole kernel, sweet white and shoepeg corn. When serving other than corn on the cob, try a combination of different corns.

 Bring the corn to a boil.

 Do not overcook.

 When preparing frozen or fresh corn cover the desired amount of corn with water and season with desired amount of butter, salt and pepper.

 Bring to a boil and boil for 7-8 minutes. Be careful not to overcook.

NOTE: When preparing canned corn remember that the corn is already cooked. Most Southerners season with a small amount of butter, salt and pepper and sugar. For best results and freshest taste when using canned corn, drain the corn and replace with an equal amount of tap water. Leftover corn is best when served as a corn casserole or corn pudding. Reheating tends to deteriorate the quality of the corn.

CAME **500** MILES OUT OF THE WAY--
WORTH IT!
---LONGVIEW, TEXAS

CREAMED CORN

1   14-ounce can creamed corn
1   cup frozen or fresh whole kernel or shoepeg corn
2   eggs
1   tablespoon self-rising flour
1   tablespoon bacon grease
4   slices bacon, fried crisp, chopped coarsely
    salt and pepper to taste

☕ Combine all the ingredients.
☕ Mix well. Do not beat.
☕ Cook in an ungreased 9x12-inch casserole dish for 30-40 minutes at 350 degrees.
    Yield: 6-8 servings.

GLAZED CARROTS

1½   pounds carrots
½   cup brown sugar
½   teaspoon salt
2   teaspoons butter
¼   cup orange marmalade
1   tablespoon Grand Marnier, optional

☕ Wash, scrape and cut carrots into 1-inch pieces.
☕ Place in saucepan and cover with water.
☕ Cook over high heat until almost done.
☕ Pour off half the water.
☕ In mixing bowl combine sugar, salt, butter, orange marmalade and Grand Marnier.

- Pour over carrots and stir gently.
- Bring back to a slow boil and cook for 4-5 minutes, stirring frequently to prevent sticking.

COOKED CABBAGE

1   **medium head cabbage**
¼   **cup butter**
1   **quart water**
      salt and pepper to taste

- Remove the outside leaves from cabbage.
- Cut in half and cut out core. Cut cabbage into bite-sized sections.
- Place in a stock pot and cover with water.
- Add half the butter, salt and pepper.
- Cook until tender, but do not overcook.
- Drain and pour balance of butter over cabbage.
- Serve hot.
Yield: 4-6 servings.

FRIED CABBAGE

Submitted by Karen Van Ness, the Blue Willow Inn's reservationist, who has endeared all of us with her genuine Louisiana mannerisms. "Ma Shea Bett," French for My Little Baby or Honey Child, is a term of endearment used often by Karen when speaking to her customers and fellow workers.

2   **small heads cabbage**
1   **pound bacon**
1   **cup chopped onions**
1   **teaspoon minced garlic**
1   **teaspoon red hot pepper**
1   **tablespoon salt (Cont.fi)**

117

 Fry the bacon until crisp and remove from pan.

 Add all other ingredients to bacon grease. Cover and cook in a heavy cast iron skillet or Dutch pot with lid.

 Remove cover and crumble bacon on top.

 Serve hot with cornbread

"Ma Shae Bett, that's fine food!"

YAMS LOUIE

4	**large sweet potatoes**
½	**cup butter**
¼	**cup granulated sugar**
¼	**cup brown sugar**
⅓	**cup orange marmalade**
⅓	**cup crushed pineapple**
¼	**cup chopped pecans**
1	**teaspoon vanilla**
1	**teaspoon cornstarch**

 Peel sweet potatoes.

 Cook covered with water in a stock pot until cooked, but firm, about 20 minutes. Cool.

 Cut into 1-inch rounds.

 Place potato rounds on sheet pan.

 In small saucepan, combine butter, sugar, vanilla, orange marmalade and crushed pineapple.

 Bring to a slow boil.

 Dissolve cornstarch in small amount of cold water. Add to saucepan and stir until thick and smooth.

 Add pecans.

 Pour mixture over potatoes.

 Cook uncovered at 350 degrees for 25-30 minutes until potatoes are tender.

CANDIED YAMS

6 **large sweet potatoes**
2 **cups granulated sugar**
2 **tablespoons vanilla flavoring**
8 **ounces butter or margarine**

 Wash and peel sweet potatoes.

 Cut into 1½-inch rounds.

 Place in a casserole or baking dish and top with sugar, vanilla and butter.

 Bake uncovered at 350 degrees for 1 hour.

HARVARD BEETS

1 **14-ounce can sliced beets, drained**
½ **cup sugar**
½ **cup apple cider vinegar**
1 **tablespoon cornstarch**
½ **teaspoon salt**

 Combine sugar, vinegar, cornstarch and salt in a saucepan.

 Cook until mixture is clear.

 Add beets to juice and cook over low heat for 20-25 minutes.
NOTE: Dissolve cornstarch in small amount of vinegar before adding to pan.

119

STEWED APPLES

Good served as a side dish with ice cream or as a
filling for apple pie.

3-4	large Granny Smith apples
1½	cups water
¼	cup brown sugar
2	tablespoons flour
¼	teaspoon salt
½	teaspoon cinnamon
¼	teaspoon nutmeg

- Wash, core, peel and slice apples.
- Combine all ingredients in a saucepan.
- Cook over low heat, simmering for 30-40 minutes until apples are tender but not too soft.

BAKED APPLES

6	Granny Smith or other tart apples
½	cup melted butter
¼	cup light brown sugar
½	teaspoon cinnamon
½	teaspoon nutmeg
¼	cup chopped pecans

- Wash and core the apples from the top.
- Do not core all the way through the apples.
- Combine butter, brown sugar, cinnamon, nutmeg and pecans in bowl and mix.
- Place apples in baking dish top up.
- Pour filling into cavities of the apples.

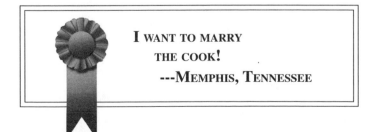

Bake at 350 degrees for 30-35 minutes until tender or cook in microwave oven for 10-15 minutes on high.
Yield: 6 servings

VIDALIA ONION CASSEROLE

If Vidalia onions are not available, Texas Sweets or Washington State Sweets will substitute.

3½	cups sliced Vidalia onions
1	5⅓-ounce can evaporated milk
1	cup bread crumbs or croutons
1	cup chicken broth
⅔	cup toasted, slivered almonds
½	cup grated Cheddar cheese
2	tablespoons melted butter
2	tablespoons flour
½	teaspoon salt

- In saucepan over medium heat, combine butter, flour, chicken broth and evaporated milk.
- Stir constantly until thick and smooth.
- Add onions. Stir in almonds and seasonings.
- Pour into buttered 1½-quart casserole dish.
- Cover with crumbs and cheese and bake at 375 degrees for 30 minutes.

I WANT TO MARRY
THE COOK!
---MEMPHIS, TENNESSEE

BAKED PINEAPPLE CASSEROLE

This recipe was submitted by Billie Harvey. The Harveys sold us the property housing the Blue Willow Inn Restaurant. For years Mrs. Harvey brought this casserole to family gatherings and church dinners. We "bribed" her for the recipe, which she had not previously shared with anyone, including family. It is always popular when served on our buffet at the Blue Willow Inn.

2	**cups grated Cheddar cheese**
1	**28-ounce can crushed pineapple**
2½	**cups Ritz cracker crumbs**
1¼	**cups granulated sugar**
1	**slick melted butter**
¼	**cup grated Cheddar cheese**

- In saucepan combine pineapple (with juice) and sugar.
- Heat until sugar is dissolved.
- In a casserole or baking dish layer pineapple, cracker crumbs, butter, and ¼ cup cheese.
- Repeat layers until you have 3-4 layers.
- Sprinkle last ¼ cup of Cheddar cheese over top of casserole.
- Bake uncovered at 350 degrees for approximately 20-25 minutes until bubbly and golden brown.

BROCCOLI CASSEROLE

2	**packages frozen broccoli**
1	**10-ounce can condensed cream of mushroom soup**
1	**cup mayonnaise**
1	**egg**

122

1   **cup grated Cheddar cheese**
½   **cup Ritz cracker crumbs**
      salt and pepper to taste

- Cook and drain broccoli.
- Mix together all ingredients except cracker crumbs and ¼ cup grated cheese.
- Pour into buttered casserole dish.
- Top with cracker crumbs and bake at 350 degrees for 30 minutes or until bubbly.
- Add remaining cheese and return to oven until melted.

SWEET POTATO SOUFFLE

3   **cups cooked fresh sweet potatoes, drained**
3   **eggs**
1   **stick melted butter**
½   **cup milk**
¼   **cup light brown sugar**
½   **cup granulated sugar**
¼   **cup raisins, optional**
¼   **teaspoon cinnamon**
1   **teaspoon vanilla**
      miniature marshmallows
      dash nutmeg

- Mash sweet potatoes with whisk or potato masher.
- Combine all ingredients and mix well.
- Pour into a 9x12-inch casserole dish and bake at 350 degrees for 25-30 minutes.
- Top with minimarshmallows or pecan topping recipe found on the next page.

123

PECAN TOPPING FOR SWEET POTATO SOUFFLE

1	cup corn flakes cereal
½	cup light brown sugar
⅓	cup melted butter
¾	cup chopped pecans

Crush corn flakes into small pieces. Add all ingredients and mix well. Spoon over sweet potato souffle. Return souffle to oven for 4-5 minutes to brown topping.

BLENDER SOUFFLE

This recipe was submitted by Frances Ann Straight. This dish can be made at the last minute or a day ahead. It never fails.

8	ounces sharp Cheddar cheese
10	slices buttered bread, crust removed
4	eggs
2	cups milk
1	teaspoon salt
½	teaspoon dry mustard

- Put half of cheese, bread, eggs and milk in blender.
- Turn on high speed until thoroughly mixed.
- Remove from blender.
- Add the rest of the ingredients to the blender and mix thoroughly.
- Combine both batches and mix well.
- Cook in greased 1½-quart casserole dish uncovered for 1 hour at 350 degrees.

Asparagus Casserole
Good for buffets or luncheons.

3   cups asparagus, with juice from cans (if frozen, add water)
1   10-ounces can condensed cream of mushroom soup
1   cup sharp Cheddar cheese, grated
1¼   cups Ritz craker crumbs
3   eggs, well beaten
2   ounces pimentos
1   ounce melted butter
      dash salt and pepper to taste

- Mix all ingredients well except butter.
- Pour into a 9x12-inch casserole dish.
- Pour melted butter over top.
- Bake uncovered at 350 degrees for 30 minutes or until light brown.

Squash Casserole

3   pounds sliced squash, cooked firm
1   medium chopped onion
½   teaspoon salt
1   10-ounce can condensed cream of chicken soup
1   cup sour cream
½   cup butter
3   eggs, slightly beaten
1   ounce bacon grease
¼   cup chopped bacon
½   cup grated Cheddar cheese, divided
2   cups Ritz cracker crumbs, divided

- Saute onions in bacon grease. (Cont.→)

- In mixing bowl add all ingredients except squash and cracker crumbs. Save ¼ cup of cheese.
- Add squash and 1½ cups cracker crumbs.
- Mix gently. Do not mash squash.
- Pour into 9x12-inch baking or casserole dish.
- Bake for 25-30 minutes at 350 degrees.
- Remove from oven and top with cracker crumbs and remaining cheese. Return to oven to brown cracker crumbs and melt cheese.

SQUASH CASSEROLE

This recipe was submitted by Rochelle Wright. She says this is the only dish her husband Kevin enjoys cooking. Cooking this dish gives Kevin full confidence that he has mastered the kitchen.

3	**cups sliced squash**
½	**teaspoon black pepper**
1	**cup chopped purple onions**
1	**stick melted butter**
2	**eggs, slightly beaten**
1	**teaspoon salt**
1	**cup milk**
1½	**cups Cheddar cheese, grated**
1	**cup herb stuffing**

- Cook squash and onions in a small skillet with 2 tablespoons of butter.
- Mix all other ingredients together. Add squash and onion.
- Pour into casserole dish.
- Bake at 350 degrees for 40 minutes.

126

CABBAGE CASSEROLE

This recipe was submitted by Sybil Allen. Billie found this dish at a church covered dish dinner. She was not sure what it was, so she stood by the dish until the owner came to pick up the dish. Billie asked Sybil, "What is this wonderful dish?" Sybil simply replied, "Oh, that's just a cabbage casserole," and she shared the recipe with Billie. The Blue Willow Inn now serves this ever popular casserole almost every Thursday with Liver and Onions.

1	head cabbage, chopped
8	slices bacon, fried crisp and chopped
1	medium onion, chopped
1	medium green bell pepper, chopped
1	can condensed cream of mushroom soup
¾	cup grated Cheddar cheese
½	cup milk
3	teaspoons bacon grease
3	slices bread, toasted and crumbled
1	stick butter, melted
1	teaspoon salt

- Cook the cabbage for 8 minutes in salted water.
- Saute onions and bell pepper in bacon grease.
- Toss bread in butter.
- Combine all ingredients except bread crumbs in casse role dish. Top with bread crumbs.
- Bake for 35 minutes at 350 degrees.

GREEN BEAN CASSEROLE

2	10-ounce cans French cut green beans, drained
1	10-ounce can condensed cream of mushroom soup
½	cup Cheddar cheese, grated
	desired amount of canned or fresh fried onion rings
	salt and black pepper to taste.

- Drain green beans.
- In a mixing bowl combine all ingredients other than onion rings. Stir to mix well.
- Pour into 9x12-inch casserole or baking dish.
- Bake 35-40 minutes at 350 degrees until bubbly.
- Top with onion rings.

NOTE: If using fresh fried onion rings, cut into thin slices and fry extra crispy. See recipe for fried onion rings.

SAVANNAH RED RICE

4	cups rice
6	slices bacon
1	medium onion, chopped
1	small bell pepper
1	28-ounce can tomatoes
1	14-ounce jar ketchup
2	ounces bacon grease
1	teaspoon Worcestershire sauce
1	teaspoon salt
1	dash black pepper
	Tabasco sauce to taste

128

- Cook and drain rice.
- Fry bacon until crisp and chop.
- Saute chopped onions and chopped bell peppers in bacon grease.
- Combine all ingredients.
- Cook in a casserole dish at 350 degrees until bubbly, ap proximately 40-50 minutes.

MACARONI & CHEESE

Macaroni and Cheese is one of the items that is served every day on the buffet at the Blue Willow Inn Restaurant. It is one of the customers' favorite dishes.

1	8-ounce package macaroni noodles
1	teaspoon vegetable shortening
1	cup grated Cheddar cheese, divided
½	cup Cheese Whiz
¾	cup milk
2	eggs, beaten
1	tablespoon mayonnaise
½	teaspoon mustard
	salt and pepper to taste

- Cook macaroni according to package directions, adding shortening to water. Do not overcook.
- Drain and combine macaroni with all other ingredients reserving ¼ cup Cheddar cheese.
- Bake uncovered, in ungreased 9x12-inch casserole for 25 to 30 minutes.
- Remove from oven and top with reserved cheese.
- Return to oven to melt.

Yield: 6-8 servings.

129

CORNBREAD DRESSING
Serve with giblet gravy and roasted turkey or baked chicken.

4	**cups cornbread crumbs**
2	**cups biscuit crumbs**
4	**eggs, slightly beaten**
2	**hard-boiled eggs**
2	**cups chicken broth**
½	**cup chopped chicken or turkey giblets**
½	**cup chopped onions**
¼	**cup chopped celery**
¼	**cup butter or margarine**
1	**teaspoon sage**
	salt and pepper to taste

- Saute the onions and celery in butter in a small skillet.
- In a large mixing bowl combine all ingredients other than chicken broth.
- Mix well.
- Add the chicken broth and mix well.
- Pour into a greased baking or casserole dish.
- Bake at 350 degrees for 35-40 minutes or until it is golden brown.

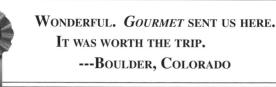

WONDERFUL. *GOURMET* SENT US HERE.
IT WAS WORTH THE TRIP.
---BOULDER, COLORADO

CHICKEN DRESSING

This recipe was submitted by Bobby Wilkes, the President of St. Simons Press, Inc., our cookbook publisher, who begged his Aunt Annie Ruth Tillman from Surrency, Georgia, to reveal the secret behind the best dressing he's ever had.

1	**5 or 6 pound hen**
1	**cup chopped onions**
1	**cup chopped celery**
16-20	**slices of toasted white bread**
⅔	**stack of Saltine crackers**
4	**eggs**
1	**chicken bouillon cube**

- Pressure cook hen covered in water approximately 45 minutes or until meat is tender.
- Reserve chicken stock.
- Debone chicken and cut into small pieces.
- Put chicken, onion, and celery in chicken stock and bring to a boil.
- Add crumbled toasted bread and Saltines. Continue to stir. Add extra crackers or bread as needed for consistency.
- Turn burner off and stir in beaten eggs. Mix well.
- Bake at 400 degrees until golden brown.

> **BOY, ARE WE FULL.**
> **ROLL US OUT THE DOOR.**
> **---FAIRFAX, VIRGINIA**

131

Mae Morrow, *manager of the Blue Willow Inn, has been with us since 1988. She started as a waitress at the restaurant in Monroe. She is an invaluable employee that has contributed significantly to our success.*

EXPERIENCING
MAIN DISHES

The Blue Willow Inn Restaurant *serves four or five meat choices and more than a dozen side dishes daily. In addition to the delectable buffet style menu, guests are always given service with a smile.*

133

ROAST BEEF

1	6 to 8-pound top round roast beef
½	teaspoon garlic salt
½	teaspoon pepper
1	cup water

- Place roast in roasting pan, fat side up.
- Season with garlic salt and pepper.
- Pour water in bottom of pan.
- Preheat oven to 425 degrees.
- Cook the first 15 minutes in 425 degree oven and turn oven down to 350 degrees.
- Continue to cook for 1½-2 hours until done.
- For medium roast beef, center should be pink but not red.

GRAVY

- Pour drippings from roasting pan into skillet.
- Over medium heat, stir in a small amount of flour and cook to brown.
- If gravy is too thick, add a small amount of water.
- When thickened let simmer 3-4 minutes.
- Gravy can be poured over sliced roast beef or served on the side.

EAT TILL YOU DROP.
Wow!
---MAINE

POT ROAST

1	6 to 8-pound beef rump roast
¼	teaspoon garlic salt
3	potatoes, peeled and diced into half pieces
4	stalks carrots, peeled and cut into half slices
3	stalks celery, cut into half slices
1	onion, sliced
2	cups water
	salt and pepper to taste
	flour

- Sprinkle roast with garlic salt.
- Combine potatoes, carrots, celery and onion.
- Place roast in center of roasting pan. Spread vegetables around pot roast.
- Add water to pan.
- Sprinkle salt and pepper as desired.
- Cook covered in 350 degree oven for 45-55 minutes.
- Remove cover and cook another 15 minutes.
- For gravy combine drippings from pot roast with ¼ - ½ cup of water in small skillet.
- Over medium heat add 2-3 tablespoons of flour to thicken.
- Allow to simmer to thicken. If too thick, add more water.
- If not thick enough, add a small amount of flour. The gravy can be poured over the pot roast or can be served as a side dish.
- A meal in itself.

Chipped Beef with White Gravy

The same recipe can be used for Chipped Ham. Simply substitute very thinly sliced ham for the roast beef.

2	**pounds very thinly sliced cooked roast beef**
¼	**cup butter**
1½	**cups milk**
1½-2	**tablespoons flour**
	toasted sliced white bread
	salt and pepper to taste

- In saucepan combine butter and flour.
- Mix to thick texture over low heat.
- Add milk. Season with salt and pepper.
- Over low heat bring to a simmer, stirring often.
- Place sliced beef in casserole dish.
- Pour white gravy over beef.
- Cover and place in a 350 degree oven for 15-20 minutes.
- Serve over crisp toast.

Yield: 6 servings.

Country Fried Steak

This has been a favorite at the Blue Willow since opening. As a child Louis grew up having this at least once a week. Great with mashed potatoes or rice.

6	**4-ounce portions of cubed beef steaks**
¼	**cup cooking oil**
½	**cup flour**
½	**sliced onion**

1	10¾ ounce can condensed cream of mushroom soup
½	cup water
	salt and pepper to taste

- In a large heavy skillet cover bottom with cooking oil.
- Turn to medium heat. Saute the onions until tender.
- Combine flour, salt and pepper.
- Using a meat mallet, tenderize the cubed beef steak.
- Dredge in flour mix and place in skillet.
- Fry each side for 4-5 minutes over medium heat. Remove from skillet.
- Add cream of mushroom soup and water to drippings from steak. Add salt and pepper to taste.
- Cook over medium heat stirring often.
- There are two methods to finish cooking the country fried steak.
- The first is to return the cooked steaks to the gravy, place onions on top and turn heat to low.
- Cover and cook for 15-18 minutes over low heat.
- The second method is to place the cooked steaks in a casserole dish and pour gravy over the dish. Cover with onions.
- Bake covered at 350 degrees for 15-20 minutes.

MEAT LOAF

This is one the favorites at the Blue Willow Inn and is usually always served on Thursdays and some Sundays. We have regular customers who come for the meat loaf every Thursday.

| 1½ | pounds ground beef |
| 3 | eggs (cont.→) |

1	cup ketchup, divided
1	cup corn flakes
3	leftover biscuits or 5-6 slices white bread
¼	cup chopped green bell peppers
¼	cup chopped onions
1	tablespoon Worcestershire sauce
	salt and pepper to taste

- In a large mixing bowl combine all ingredients reserving ½ cup ketchup. Mix well.
- Dump out of the mixing bowl onto a sheet pan.
- Work as if kneading bread several times. Mold into a loaf.
- Place in loaf pan and bake at 350 degrees uncovered for 30-40 minutes until done.
- Remove from oven and top with remaining ketchup.

EASY OVEN STEW

This recipe was submitted by Nellie Baines.

2	pounds stew beef
2	tablespoons flour
1	teaspoon salt
1	teaspoon paprika
2	tablespoons cooking oil
4	small onions
4	small carrots
4	small potatoes
1	cup sliced celery
1	dash pepper
1	14-ounce can Hunts tomato sauce

2   **cups water**

- ☛ Sprinkle beef with flour. Add paprika.
- ☛ Toss with oil in 3-quart casserole dish.
- ☛ Bake uncovered at 400 degrees for 30 minutes stirring once while baking.
- ☛ Add vegetables, salt and pepper.
- ☛ Pour tomato sauce and water over vegetables.
- ☛ Cover and bake at 350 degrees for 1¾ hours.

BEEF STROGANOFF

3	**pounds cubed sirloin tip roast, or ground beef**
¼	**cup cooking sherry**
1	**10-ounce can condensed cream of mushroom soup**
¾	**cup fresh mushrooms, sliced (or 2 small jars)**
1	**chopped onion**
1	**cup sour cream**
¼	**cup butter**
	salt and pepper to taste

- ☛ In a large heavy skillet combine butter, sherry, onions and beef.
- ☛ Saute beef and onions until done and tender.
- ☛ Add mushrooms and continue to cook 2-3 more minutes.
- ☛ Add all other ingredients and turn heat down so that mixture simmers only.
- ☛ Stir occasionally and cook covered for 15-20 minutes.
- ☛ Serve over cooked noodles.
Yield: 6 servings

LASAGNA

This recipe was submitted by Joanna Lewis who is a waitress at the Blue Willow Inn Restaurant. This is one of Billie's favorite dishes, and Joanna bakes lasagna for Billie on her birthday, Christmas, and boss's day. Although lasagna is not traditionally Southern, it is included in the cookbook because it is so wonderful.

2	12-ounce cans tomato paste
1	12-ounce can tomato puree
3	cloves garlic
¼	cup olive oil
1½	pounds ground beef
1	pound bulk Italian sausages
3	teaspoons sweet basil, or 3 fresh sweet basil leaves
2	teaspoons oregano
1	teaspoon garlic powder
½	teaspoon salt
½	teaspoon black pepper
2	tablespoons parsley flakes
5	cups water
2	16-ounce packages Ricotta cheese
2	12-ounce packages grated Mozzarella cheese
1	8-ounce package grated Parmesan cheese
½	cup fresh cut parsley
¼	cup black pepper
1	pound lasagna noodles, cooked for 8-10 minutes
2	tablespoons of olive oil, drained

- Brown garlic in olive oil in large dutch kettle.
- Add tomato paste and tomato puree and stir.
- Add water, sweet basil, oregano, parsley, garlic powder,

salt and ½ teaspoon pepper.

- In separate pan saute the sausage and hamburger until half cooked.   Drain the grease.
- Add the meat and ¼ cup grated Parmesan cheese to the sauce. Mix well.
- Bring to a boil then simmer for 2½ to 3 hours until thick.
- Mix Ricotta cheese with parsley and black pepper.
- In a 13x9-inch pan, spoon the sauce to cover the bottom of pan.
- Lay lasagna noodles lengthwise overlapping just a bit.
- Spread sauce over noodles.
- Sprinkle Mozzarella cheese over sauce.
- Then spoon Ricotta mixture and cottage cheese over mixture.
- Sprinkle Parmesan cheese.
- Arrange the next layer of lasagna noodles across the width of the pan.
- Repeat the order of sauce and cheeses. This should make 3-4 layers of lasgana in baking dish.
- Bake at 350 degrees for 45-55 minutes.
- Allow to cool for 10-20 minutes before serving.

BEST FOOD I EVER HAD.
---ROME, ITALY

LIVER AND ONIONS

Liver and onions is served at the Blue Willow Inn every Thursday for lunch and supper. It seems like no one ever cooks liver at home any more, and we have regular customers who love it and some who would never touch it.

> **desired number of pieces of beef liver**
> **flour**
> **salt and pepper to taste**
> **cooking oil**
> **sliced onion**

- In a heavy skillet pour a small amount of cooking oil and turn heat to medium.
- Saute sliced onions until tender and slightly brown.
- Remove onions from skillet.
- Add salt and pepper to flour.
- Coat each side of the liver with flour.
- Pour enough oil in skillet to cover bottom. Place liver in hot oil.
- When red juices are flowing from the top turn over liver.
- Add a little more oil if needed.
- Cook for 2-3 minutes and turn again.
- Do not overcook as it will make liver tough. When done remove from heat and smother with onions.

BAKED PORK CHOPS AND RICE

6	**pork chops**
1	**cup uncooked rice**
3	**cups hot water**

1   **teaspoon salt**
1   **teaspoon pepper**
1   **large onion, chopped**
1   **large green bell pepper, sliced in rings**
1   **10¾-ounce can condensed cream of mushroom soup**

- Trim fat off pork chops and brown in skillet on both sides in small amount of oil.
- In shallow baking dish, mix rice, water, salt, pepper, onion and undiluted soup.
- Add green pepper.
- Place pork chops on mixture.
- Cover with foil and bake for 45 minutes to 1 hour at 350 degrees.

BAKED PORK CHOPS

Simple and easy. A great dish!

6   **center cut pork chops**
1   **can Campbell's golden cream of mushroom soup**
⅔   **cup water**
      pepper to taste
      garlic salt to taste

- Lightly grease casserole dish.
- Place pork chops in casserole dish and cover with Campbell's golden cream of mushroom soup. Add water.
- Cover and cook for 30-40 minutes at 350 degrees until done.

FRIED PORK CHOPS

A customer from Richmond, Virginia said, "These are good enough to make you want to slap your momma!" After eating these pork chops, though, you don't have to slap your momma--just enjoy!

6   **5 or 6-ounce center cut pork chops**
1-1½   **cups flour**
       salt and pepper to taste
       cooking oil

- Wash pork chops in water.
- Combine flour, salt and pepper.
- Dredge pork chops in flour.
- Pour enough oil in a large heavy skillet to cover bottom of skillet.   Turn heat to medium.
- Place pork chops in skillet.   Do not crowd.
- Cook until red juices are showing on the top side.
- Turn over and add a little more oil if necessary to prevent sticking.
- Cook for 8-10 minutes until golden brown.
- Make sure the inside is done.   Pork should always be cooked done and not pink inside.

GRAVY:
- After cooking pork chops add ¼ cup water and 3 tablespoons of flour to drippings.
- Cook over medium to high heat while stirring to bring to a consistency of gravy.
- If too thick, add a little more water.   If too thin, add a little more flour.
- Cook over low to medium heat for 10-15 minutes.
- The gravy can be served as a side dish with the pork chops

or the pork chops can be returned to the skillet and covered with gravy.

Yield: 6 servings

PORK TENDERLOIN

A favorite of Elton Wright, Business Manager for the Blue Willow Inn.

1	**pork tenderloin, cut in half**
2	**tablespoons yellow mustard**
2	**teaspoons thyme**
1	**teaspoon ground ginger**
1	**teaspoon salt**
½	**teaspoon minced garlic**
½	**teaspoon cracked black pepper**
½	**cup port wine**
¼	**cup soy sauce**
2	**tablespoons Wesson oil**
2	**tablespoons currant jelly**

- For marinate, mix together mustard, thyme, ginger, salt, garlic and black pepper. Spread over tenderloins.
- Mix port wine and soy sauce. Pour over tenderloins.
- Cover and refrigerate for 24 hours.
- In heavy skillet heat oil.
- Reserve marinate from tenderloin.
- When oil is hot brown both sides of tenderloin, fat side down to start.
- Remove tenderloin from skillet and place on roasting pan coated with Pam spray. (cont. →)

- Combine marinate with drippings in skillet and pour over loins.
- Cook covered at 375 degrees for 5 minutes per pound.
- Uncover and cook for an additional 7 minutes per pound until done.
- Combine drippings from roasting pan with 2 tablespoons currant jelly.   Serve with meat.

PORK ROAST

1	**3 or 4-pound Boston butt pork roast**
½	**teaspoon garlic salt**
1	**teaspoon black pepper**
1	**cup water**

- Place pork roast in roasting pan fat down.
- Sprinkle with garlic salt and black pepper.
- Pour 1 cup of water into roasting pan.
- Cook 1½ to 2 hours at 375 degrees until done.
- Pork should be cooked completely through and not be pink.

PORK GRAVY
- Place drippings from cooked roast in skillet.
- Add enough flour over medium heat to thicken.
- To stretch gravy if drippings are not sufficient add a small amount of water.
- Season with garlic salt and pepper.
- This is a rich gravy and a little goes a long way.   Good over baked sweet potatoes with butter.

146

GRITS LASAGNA

This recipe was submitted by Marie Van Dyke.

7	cups water
1	teaspoon salt
2	cups quick cook grits, uncooked OR 2 cups instant Pollenta, uncooked
1	pound lean ground pork (not sausage)
1	cup fresh, chopped mushrooms
1	30-ounce jar Ragu Thick & Hearty spaghetti sauce
1½	cups shredded sharp Cheddar cheese
1½	cups shredded Jack or Mozzarella cheese

- In large saucepan bring water and salt to a boil.
- Gradually add grits while stirring.
- Reduce heat and simmer while stirring for 5 minutes until grits are thick and pull away from the sides of the pan.
- Pour grits into a 15½x10½-inch jelly roll pan or sided cookie sheet.
- Spread evenly to cover bottom of pan.
- Let stand 30 minutes until cool and firm. Cut into approximately 3-inch squares.
- Cook the ground pork in a large skillet until browned, stirring to crumble. Drain.
- Combine pork, mushrooms and spaghetti sauce and mix well.
- Arrange half of the grit squares in the bottom of a 13x9x2-inch baking pan (coated with Pam spray).
- Spoon half of the sauce over the grits spreading to the edges.
- Sprinkle half of the cheeses. Repeat layers. (cont. →)

147

 Bake at 450 degrees for 15-20 minutes until hot and bubbly.

 Let stand for 10 minutes before cutting.
Yield: 6-8 servings.

SAUSAGE AND EGG CASSEROLE
Good quiche for breakfasts or brunches! Men also enjoy this dish.

1	**pound mild sausages**
1	**pound hot sausages**
3	**cups croutons, unseasoned or toasted bread crumbs**
4	**cups sharp grated Cheddar cheese**
18	**eggs**
6	**cups milk**
1	**tablespoon salt**
1	**tablespoon mustard**
2	**tablespoons Worcestershire sauce**
1	**can condensed cream of mushroom soup**

 Cook sausage and drain thoroughly.

 Stir eggs to break yolks.

 Mix all ingredients together. Stir. Do not beat.

 Refrigerate overnight to season.

 Pour into casserole dish.

 Cook at 350 degrees until firm, approximately 45-50 minutes.

FRESH HAM

1	**8-10 pound fresh ham**
1	**cup water**
	salt and pepper to taste

148

Place ham on roasting pan, fat down.

Pour water into pan.

Cook uncovered for 2½-3 hours at 375 degrees until fully done.

Slice and serve.

SUGAR CURED HAM

Sugar cured hams are fully cooked. Although it is not necessary to heat the ham, when serving this meat as a main course, it is desirable in order to enjoy the full flavor of the ham.

Place on a roasting dish and place in a 350 degree oven.

Cook for 1 to 1½ hours depending on the size of ham.

Serve hot.

NOTE: When finished eating the ham, save the ham bone to season greens or beans. Old Southern cooks would almost kill for ham bones.

GRILLED HAM

desired amount of sliced, cooked ham
cooking oil

Coat the bottom of heavy skillet with a small amount of cooking oil.

Place ham in skillet and turn on medium heat.

Cook until brown and turn over and cook other side.

If ham sticks add a small amount of oil.

NOTE: Grilled ham is great with grits and eggs or in biscuits. Also, makes a great sandwich. While grilling the
(cont. →)

149

ham place Swiss or American cheese on top to melt. Build *your sandwich with mayonnaise, mustard, lettuce and to-mato with white or brown bread.*

Hawaiian Grilled Ham

6	**5 or 6-ounce slices cooked ham**
6	**pineapple rings**
6	**cherries, whole with stems**
¼	**cup pineapple juice**
¼	**cup light brown sugar**
¼	**cup butter**

- In a small saucepan combine pineapple juice, butter and sugar.
- Heat to dissolve and thicken, stirring often.
- Coat each piece of ham with the glaze.
- Place the ham side by side in a heavy skillet and turn to medium heat.
- Cook until glaze begins to bubble in skillet.
- Turn over ham and place pineapple ring and cherry on top of each piece.
- Pour remaining glaze over ham.
- Cook for 3-4 minutes.
- Remove and serve hot.

WE'LL BE BACK!
---SAN FRANCISCO, CALIFORNIA

HAM BROCCOLI CASSEROLE
Good meat substitute casserole for buffet line.

½   cup mayonnaise
2   cups broccoli florets, fresh or frozen
1½   cups sharp Cheddar cheese, shredded
1   cup chopped ham
1½   cups noodles, macaroni or corkscrew, cooked and
       drained
⅛   cup chopped green bell peppers
¼   cup milk
½   cup seasoned croutons

- Mix all ingredients except ½ cup cheese and croutons. Spoon into a 9x12-inch casserole dish.
- Sprinkle with remaining cheese and croutons.
- Bake at 350 degrees for 25-30 minutes until bubbly.

CHEESY HAM POTATO CASSEROLE

2   pounds cooked ham
6   medium, cooked potatoes
       OR
12   small new red potatoes, cooked with skin on, cut in
       half

CHEESE SAUCE
2   cups milk, divided
¼   cup all-purpose flour
½   cup Cheese Whiz

½   **cup grated Cheddar cheese**
½   **teaspoon salt**
1   **dash black pepper**

- Cut ham and potatoes into ¾-inch cubes.
- If using new red potatoes do not dice.
- Prepare cheese sauce by mixing 1½ cups milk with cheese, Cheese Whiz, salt and pepper in heavy saucepan.
- Cook over low heat stirring constantly until cheese melts and sauce simmers.
- Mix ¼ cup flour with ½ cup milk until smooth.
- Stir into cheese mixture until thickened.
- Simmer for 20 minutes stirring constantly.
- Place ham and potatoes in casserole dish.
- Pour cheese sauce over ham and potatoes to cover.
- Bake uncovered for 20-25 minutes until cheese begins to brown.

SOUTHERN FRIED CHICKEN

Southern Fried Chicken is served with every meal at the Blue Willow Inn. It is always a favorite. Savannah Magazine called our chicken "to die for fried chicken."

1   **broiler-fryer chicken, cut into 8 pieces**
1   **quart water**
1½   **cups flour**
½   **teaspoon salt**
½   **teaspoon black pepper**
       cooking oil

- In a large, deep heavy skillet heat enough oil to cover chicken.

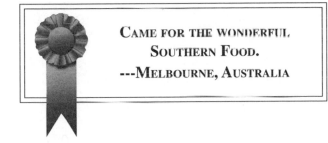 Wash chicken thoroughly and remove excess fat.

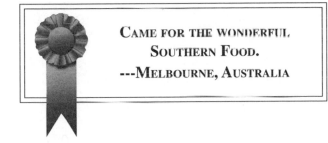 Cover chicken in a bowl with 1 quart of water. Allow to sit for 3-4 minutes.

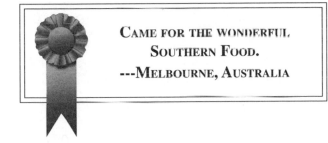 Mix flour, salt and pepper.

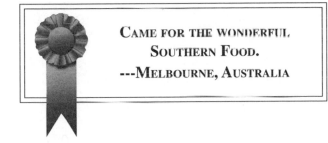 Remove chicken from water shaking off only part of the water. Chicken should be moist.

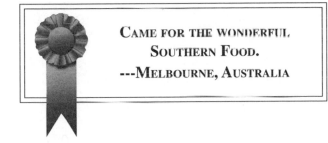 Dredge in flour mixture.

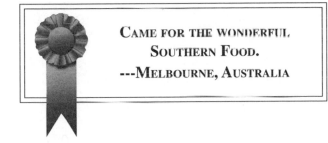 Place in hot oil and cook uncovered.

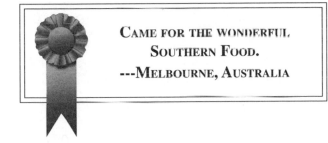 Make sure hot oil covers the chicken. Do not crowd the chicken.

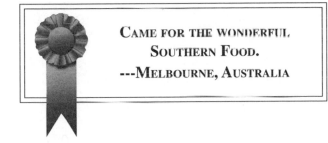 Turn once to cook and brown other side.

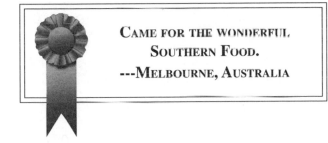 Remove from oil when done and drain on paper towel.

> CAME FOR THE WONDERFUL
> SOUTHERN FOOD.
> ---MELBOURNE, AUSTRALIA

BAKED CHICKEN

1   **8-piece cut up chicken**
¼   **cup butter**
      salt and pepper to taste

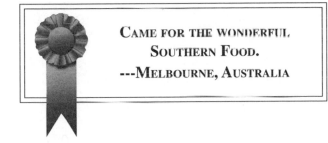 Remove excess fat and wash chicken.

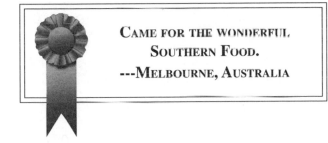 Place on lightly buttered baking pan skin up.

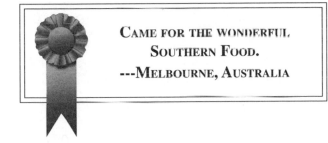 Baste with butter and season with salt and pepper.

 Bake uncovered 45-50 minutes uncovered until golden brown.

153

CHICKEN POT PIE

1	14-ounce can early June peas, drained
1½	cups cooked chicken
½	cup cooked, diced potatoes
½	cup celery, chopped and cooked
½	cup carrots, sliced
1¼	cups chicken broth
1	10¾-ounce can condensed cream of chicken soup
6	biscuits, cut in half
	salt and pepper to taste

 Mix all ingredients together except ½ cup of chicken broth and biscuits.

Place bottom halves of biscuits on bottom of 10x13-inch casserole dish.

Pour mixture over biscuits.

Place top half of biscuits on top and press down.

Pour remaining chicken broth on top of recipe for moistness.

Cook for 30-40 minutes at 350 degrees until biscuits are golden brown and pie is bubbly.

Yield: 6-8 servings.

GOD HAS BLESSED THE COOKS!
---MONTICELLO, GEORGIA

CHICKEN DIVINE

3	pounds cooked boneless chicken
3	pounds cooked broccoli
2	10-ounce cans condensed cream of chicken soup
¾	cup mayonnaise
⅔	cup milk
2½	cups grated Cheddar cheese (or 1¼ cup cheese sauce)
1	tablespoon curry powder
3	tablespoons lemon juice, concentrated
⅓	cup grated Cheddar cheese for topping
2	cups bread crumbs or Ritz cracker crumbs

- Combine soup, mayonnaise, milk, 2½ cups cheese, lemon juice and curry powder.
- Mix well. Do not beat.
- Layer casserole or baking pan with broccoli then chicken.
- Add sauce mixture and spread evenly over chicken.
- Add bread or cracker crumbs.
- Cook at 350 degrees for 30-40 minutes.
- Remove from oven and top with ⅓ cup grated cheddar cheese.
- Melt cheese.
- Serve hot.

CHICKEN AND RICE

1	broiler-fryer chicken
4	cups cooked rice (cont. →)

½   cup chicken broth
1   10¾-ounce can condensed cream of chicken soup
2   hard-boiled eggs
½   cup chopped celery
2   tablespoons butter
¼   cup milk
¼   cup sliced mushrooms

 Wash chicken and cook whole in stock pot covered with water. Include giblets.

 When done, remove chicken from broth and cool chicken in cold water.

 Remove bones, fat and skin. Tear into bite-size pieces.

 Coarsely chop giblets.

 In small skillet saute celery in butter. When celery is almost tender add mushrooms and saute together.

 Combine all ingredients and mix well.

 Place in casserole or baking dish and bake at 350 degrees for 30-40 minutes. Mixture should be almost too moist when placed in oven as it will be too dry if not overly moist. For better flavor cook the rice in the chicken broth after you have boiled the chicken.

OPAL'S CHICKEN CASSEROLE

This recipe was submitted by Opal Wilson who worked for Louis and Billie for several years off and on. She worked as a cashier, a hostess and also as a manager. Opal brought to the restaurant many years of experience in cooking and operating restaurants as she had previously owned her own restaurant on two occasions. Opal got a lot of pleasure doing little things for people. She now resides in Beaufort, South Carolina and is enjoying retirement. We all miss her dearly.

4	cups cooked boneless chicken
1	cup chicken broth
1	can condensed cream of mushroom soup
1	can condensed cream of celery soup
⅔	cup milk
1	12-ounce package Jiffy cornbread mix
	salt and pepper to taste

 Place chicken in baking or casserole dish.

 Mix all ingredients other than cornbread mix.

 Pour over chicken.

 Top with cornbread mix.

 Bake at 350 degrees for 40-50 minutes until bubbly and brown.

CHICKEN CASSEROLE

This recipe was submitted by Becky Young. When Becky's husband, Kenneth, was the pastor of the Monroe, Georgia Church of God, the Youngs came every Sunday for lunch and usually brought a crowd with them. One day Becky gave Billie this Chicken Casserole recipe and said she thought it would go well on the buffet. She was right! Thank you, Becky.

8	chicken breasts, cooked and deboned
1	cup sour cream
1	10-ounce can condensed cream of chicken soup
1	cup chicken broth
1	10-ounce can condensed cream of mushroom soup
2	stacks Ritz crackers
1½	sticks melted butter (cont. →)

-  Mix together sour cream, cream of chicken soup, cream of mushroom soup and chicken broth.
-  Place chicken in baking dish. Pour mixture over chicken.
-  Top with cracker crumbs and butter.
-  Bake at 350 degrees for 35-40 minutes until crackers are brown.

CHICKEN TETRAZZINI

¼	**cup coarsely chopped green peppers**
¼	**cup coarsely chopped onions**
½	**cup sliced mushrooms**
1	**heaping tablespoon pimentos**
⅛	**tablespoon garlic powder**
¼	**cup chopped black olives**
1½	**cups cooked and deboned chicken**
1	**small package vermicelli (spaghetti) noodles**
½	**cup milk**
¼	**Cheese Whiz**
1	**10¾-ounce can condensed cream of chicken soup**
¾	**cup grated Cheddar cheese**

-  Cook vermicelli noodles in chicken broth.
-  Saute peppers, onions, mushrooms, pimentos and black olives in butter.
-  Add all ingredients except ¼ cup grated cheese to spaghetti noodles. Mix well.
-  Pour into a 10x13-inch casserole dish.
-  Cook at 350 degrees for 30-40 minutes until bubbly.
-  Top with remaining grated Cheddar cheese. Mixture should be moist.

Yield: 6-8 servings.

LITE & EASY GREEK CHICKEN

This recipe was submitted by Marie Van Dyke. It goes great over angel hair pasta or rice.

1	broiler-fryer chicken, cut into pieces
4	tablespoons olive oil
2	tablespoons minced fresh garlic
½	cup sliced black olives
½	cup sliced green olives
2	teaspoons basil
2	teaspoons oregano
2	16-ounce cans whole tomatoes, slightly crushed
¼	cup fresh parsley
	juice of 1 fresh lemon
	salt and pepper to taste

In a large skillet saute in olive oil the garlic and chicken until chicken is browned on both sides.

Add the canned tomatoes with the juice and all other ingredients except the lemon and parsley.

Squeeze the lemon over the pan and add the fresh parsley.

Cover and simmer for 45-50 minutes.

EXCELLENT. ALOHA NIU.
---HONOLULU, HAWAII

GRILLED LEMON CHICKEN

This recipe was submitted by Sandi McClain who is the manager of the Blue Willow Inn Gift Shop. She was also the decorator for Blue Willow's Magnolia Hall Catering Facility. At a recent ladies luncheon and fashion show at Magnolia Hall, Sandi's recipe for Grilled Lemon Chicken was a hit! It's easy and delicious!

6	**4-ounce boneless chicken breasts**
¾	**cup flour**
	lemon pepper
½	**tablespoon lemon juice**
	stick butter

- Rinse chicken breasts. Pound 2-3 times with a meat mallet.
- Dredge in flour.
- In large, heavy skillet melt butter.
- Place chicken breasts in skillet and sprinkle generously with lemon pepper.
- Cook over medium heat on each side 6 minutes again sprinkling with lemon pepper when turning chicken.
- Turn skillet down to low heat and add lemon juice.
- Cook for 5 minutes.

Yield: 6 servings.

ORANGE PECAN GLAZED CHICKEN AND WILD RICE

This is a good dish for special occasions and holidays. It's easy but festive.

1	**cut up broiler-fryer chicken**
1	**package Uncle Ben's Long Grain Wild rice**

½   **cup melted butter**
½   **cup orange marmalade**
¼   **cup frozen concentrated orange juice**
1   **teaspoon cornstarch**
½   **cup chopped pecans**
     chicken broth, if available
     salt and pepper to taste

- Cook rice according to directions on package.
- If chicken broth is available substitute chicken broth for water for the rice.
- Place chicken on baking pan.
- Baste with butter and season with salt and pepper.
- Bake at 350 degrees for 25-30 minutes.
- In saucepan combine balance of butter, orange marma lade and orange juice.
- Bring to boil.
- Dissolve cornstarch in small amount of water. Slowly add enough cornstarch to thicken while stirring.
- Add pecans.
- Place cooked rice in 9x13 casserole dish. Arrange baked chicken on top of rice.
- Pour orange glaze over chicken.
- Return to oven to cook 12-15 minutes or until glaze be gins to brown.

Yield: 4-6 servings

NOTE: Cornish game hens can be substituted for the chicken. Either cut in half lengthwise or cook whole. Follow same directions as for chicken.

FRIED CHICKEN LIVERS

2   cups water
1-2   cups flour
       desired number of chicken livers
       cooking oil
       salt and pepper to taste

 Heat oil in large deep skillet.

 Wash chicken livers and cover with water.

 Combine flour, salt and pepper.

 Remove livers one at a time from water shaking excess water and dredge in flour.

 Place in hot oil one at a time.

 Gently stir frequently while cooking.

 Cook for 8-12 minutes until golden brown turning once.

 When done, remove from grease and drain on paper towel.
NOTE: Chicken livers tend to pop grease. If you have a skillet screen, place it over the pan to prevent popping grease from burning you.

ROAST TURKEY
Serve with cornbread dressing and giblet gravy.

1   12 to 14-pound tom turkey
¼   cup butter
1   teaspoon salt
½   teaspoon pepper
1   cup water

 Since most turkeys are sold frozen allow turkey to thaw

2-3 days in the refrigerator before cooking.

- Remove giblets and neck bones from cavity. Save for giblet gravy.
- Rinse turkey with cold water. Place in large roasting pan.
- Mix butter, salt and pepper.
- Pour over turkey.
- Pour 1 cup of water in bottom of roasting pan.
- Bake for 3-4 hours in 350 degrees oven until fully cooked.
- Reserve drippings for giblet gravy (see recipe).

John's Quail

This recipe was submitted by John Lowe and was served to Gertrude H. Lowe, age 90, on Easter Sunday 1996, with angel biscuits, creamy gravy, baked sweet potatoes, plum jam and green salad. There is a picture of John and his mother on page 42.

split quail breasts
buttermilk
flour
thyme
black pepper
butter
apple slices

- Spilt the quail breasts and soak them in buttermilk.
- Season flour to taste with thyme and black pepper.
- Put soaked quail pieces in container with 2 cups seasoned flour and shake.
- Brown in butter in skillet (215 degrees).
- Place quail on top of raw apple slices in an uncovered slightly greased baking pan.
- Place in a 350 degrees preheated oven for 30 minutes. (cont. →)

 Serve with creamy gravy and hot biscuits with plum or cherry preserves.

Creamy Gravy for John's Quail

1½	**cups spring water**
4	**tablespoons white flour**
5	**tablespoons drippings from John's Quail recipe**

 Put 1½ cups spring water and 4 tablespoons of white flour in container with tight top that can be shaken vigorously.

 Shake until mixture is foamy and then shake again just before pouring into the skillet used to brown the quail which now contains 5 tablespoons of drippings.

 Turn heat on medium high while continually agitating mixture with a straight edge spatula until it has boiled about 1½ minutes or desired thickness is attained.

 Pour over quail just before serving.

NOTE: For real brown gravy, brown the flour in the oven before mixing.

SEAFOOD GUMBO

3	**tablespoons butter**
1	**cup chopped celery**
1	**pound fresh or frozen okra**
2	**12-ounce cans tomatoes**
2	**pounds shelled and cleaned shrimp**
1	**pint raw oysters**
2	**onions, chopped**
1	**green bell pepper, chopped**

1	10-ounce can tomato sauce
3	quarts water
1	ounce crab meat
	drops Tabasco sauce
	cooked rice
	salt and pepper to taste

- 🍴 In a large heavy skillet saute onions, bell pepper and celery in butter until tender.
- 🍴 Add okra and cook until tender.
- 🍴 In a 6-quart stock pot combine water, tomatoes, tomato sauce and seasonings.
- 🍴 Cook on medium heat for 30 minutes.
- 🍴 Add sauteed vegetables to pot and continue cooking on low heat for two hours, stirring occasionally.
- 🍴 Add raw shrimp and cook 15 more minutes.
- 🍴 Add crabmeat and oysters and cook another 15 minutes. Serve over hot rice.

  NOTE: For thicker gumbo dissolve 1-2 teaspoons of corn starch in 1 tablespoon of water and add to pot and stir to thicken.

SEAFOOD CRABMEAT CASSEROLE

2	cups coarsely chopped celery
1	8-ounce can sliced water chestnuts
½	cup onions, chopped
1	pepper, medium chopped green
12	ounces Sea Legs imitation crabmeat
2½	ounces pimentos
1	cup mayonnaise (cont. →)

4   **eggs, hard-boiled and sliced**
½   **teaspoon salt**
½   **teaspoon paprika**
½   **cup buttered bread crumbs**

- In a large bowl combine all ingredients except bread crumbs.
- Toss gently.
- Pour into greased 9x12-inch casserole dish.
- Top with buttered bread crumbs.
- Bake at 350 degrees for 30 minutes or until bubbly.

CRAB (SEA LEGS) CASSEROLE

12   **ounces Sea Legs brand imitation crabmeat**
8   **ounces sliced water chestnuts**
½   **cup chopped onions**
1   **cup mayonnaise**
4   **hard-boiled eggs**
1   **small green bell pepper, chopped**
2   **cups celery, chopped coarsely**
½   **teaspoon salt**
½   **teaspoon paprika**
½   **cup bread crumbs, buttered**

- In a large mixing bowl combine all ingredients except bread crumbs. Mix lightly.
- Pour into greased 9x12-inch casserole dish.
- Sprinkle top with buttered bread crumbs.
- Bake at 350 degrees for 30 minutes or until golden brown and bubbly.

SEAFOOD AU GRATIN

1½	cups cooked and peeled shrimp
1	8-ounce can lump crabmeat
8	ounces cooked flounder or turbot
2	cups milk, divided
¼	cup all-purpose flour
½	cup Cheese Whiz
½	cup grated Cheddar cheese
½	teaspoon salt
	dash black pepper

- Mix 1½ cups milk with cheese, Cheese Whiz, salt and pepper in heavy saucepan.
- Cook over low heat stirring constantly until cheese melts and sauce simmers.
- Mix ¼ cup flour with ½ cup milk until smooth.
- Stir into cheese mixture until thickened.
- Simmer for 20 minutes, stirring constantly.
- In mixing bowl combine shrimp, fish and crabmeat. Stir to break apart fish and crabmeat.
- Transfer seafood to casserole dish or au gratin dishes.
- Pour cheese sauce over seafood to cover.
- Bake uncovered 20-25 minutes in a 350 degree oven until cheese begins to brown.

> **INCREDIBLE!**
> ---MADRID, SPAIN

TUNA CASSEROLE
This is Louis's favorite casserole.

1   6-ounce can solid white tuna in water
1   package cooked and drained seashell noodles
1   10-ounce can condensed cream of mushroom soup
1   cup grated Cheddar cheese
½   teaspoon salt
25   Ritz crackers, crumbled into crumbs

- Mix together except for grated ½ cup cheese and cracker crumbs.
- Bake at 350 degrees for 30 minutes.
- Top with cracker crumbs and remaining grated cheese.
- Melt cheese.

SAVANNAH SHRIMP & RICE
This recipe was given to Billie by one of her neighbors when she lived on Burnside Island in Savannah. Over the years this has become one of her specialties.

2   pounds cooked rice
1   pound cooked shrimp, peeled and deveined
1   10¾-ounce can Campbell's condensed cream of mushroom soup
1   small onion, chopped
1   small green bell pepper, chopped
1   tablespoon butter
      teaspoon curry powder
      cup grated Cheddar cheese
      salt and pepper to taste

- Saute onion and bell pepper in butter.
- In mixing bowl combine all of the ingredients except cheese, mixing well.
- Pour into a 9x12-inch baking dish.
- Bake at 350 degrees for 25-30 minutes until bubbly.
- Top with cheese and serve.

Yield: 8 servings

SALMON CROQUETTES

1	**14.75-ounce can salmon, packed in water**
2	**eggs**
1	**heaping tablespoon chopped onion**
¼	**cup flour**
	cooking oil

- In mixing bowl combine salmon, eggs, onions and flour.
- Mix well.
- Roll into balls the size of golf balls. If the mix is too loose, add more flour and mix well.
- Pat into rounds with center ½-inch thick.
- In heavy skillet pour enough cooking oil to cover bottom of skillet.
- Cook salmon patties on medium heat for 7-8 minutes on each side adding oil when necessary to cover bottom of skillet.

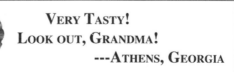

VERY TASTY!
LOOK OUT, GRANDMA!
---ATHENS, GEORGIA

BAKED FLOUNDER

desired number of 6-8-ounce flounder fillets
melted butter
salt
lemon pepper
sliced lemon
sliced almonds, optional
fresh parsley sprig

- Lightly butter the inside of a baking pan. Place flounder fillets on pan.
- Using a pastry or butter brush baste the flounder with butter.
- Sprinkle with salt and lemon pepper to taste.
- Bake at 350 degrees for 12-15 minutes depending on thickness of the fillets.
- Remove from oven and garnish with parsley and lemon.
- For baked flounder almondine lightly toast slivered almonds. Sprinkle almonds on top of fillets before baking. *NOTE: Turbot fillets can be substituted for flounder.*

FRIED CATFISH

Serve with slaw, french fries, hush puppies and sweetened iced tea.

desired number of 4-8-ounce catfish
cornmeal
salt
water
cooking oil

-  If catfish is fresh remove head, gut and clean.
-  Place in bowl of cold water and salt the water.
-  Allow to sit for 10-15 minutes.
-  Remove from water and blot excess water.
-  Heat cooking oil in heavy skillet using enough oil to cover fish.
-  Dredge fish in cornmeal, salted to taste.
-  Place fish in oil, cooking on each side for 6-10 minutes depending on the size of the catfish.
-  Drain on paper towel.

SCALLOPED OYSTERS

1	**pint oysters**
1	**pint milk**
2	**cups cracker crumbs**
1	**tablespoon Worcestershire sauce**
¼	**teaspoon salt**
½	**cup melted butter**

-  Layer oysters and cracker crumbs in ungreased baking dish.
-  Dot layer with butter and repeat.
-  Pour milk on top.
-  Bake at 350 degrees for 40 minutes.

WE LOVE THIS PLACE!
---OVERLAND PARK, KANSAS

171

Southern Fried Oysters

1	cup self-rising cornmeal
1	cup self-rising flour
¼	teaspoon red hot pepper, optional
2	eggs
2	tablespoons milk
24	ounces fresh select oysters, drained
	vegetable oil, for frying

- Combine cornmeal, flour and red pepper, mixing well.
- Combine eggs and milk, beating well with a fork.
- Dip oysters in egg mixture and dredge in flour mixture.
- Fry in vegetable oil at 375 degrees for 2-3 minutes until golden brown.

Fried Fatback (or Streak O' Lean)

fatback or streak o'lean
cooking oil
water

- Thinly slice the desired amount of fatback or streak o'lean.
- Soak in water for 30-40 minutes.
- Shake off excess water and fry in oil over medium heat. Fry until crisp but not hard.
- Drain on paper towel.
- Serve with white gravy.

EXPERIENCING
BREADS AND ROLLS

The Blue Willow Inn *offers some of the finest biscuits, muffins, and cornbread found in the South.*

173

BUTTERMILK BISCUITS

2	**cups self-rising flour**
1	**dash salt**
½	**teaspoon sugar**
3	**tablespoons shortening**
½	**cup buttermilk**
½	**cup sweet milk**
1	**tablespoon water**
2	**tablespoons melted butter**

- Sift flour, salt and sugar together into mixing bowl.
- Cut in shortening until mixture is coarse.
- Add buttermilk, milk, water and 1 tablespoon butter.
- Mix lightly until mixed well. Do not overmix. Pour mixture onto a lightly floured surface.
- Knead dough two to three times. Knead several more times only if using biscuits for sandwich biscuits.
- With floured hands pat out dough to approximately ½-inch thickness.
- Cut with biscuit cutter. Do not twist cutter.
- Bake at 475 degrees for 10-12 minutes until golden brown.
- Brush with butter after removing from oven.

ANGEL BISCUITS

4	**cups flour**
3	**teaspoons baking powder**
1	**teaspoon salt**
1	**package active dry yeast**

2	cups buttermilk
¼	cup sugar
1	teaspoon baking soda
½	cup shortening
2	teaspoons warm water

 Sift the flour, sugar, baking powder, soda and salt together.

 Cut in shortening.

 Soften yeast in warm water.   Stir until dissolved.

 Mix with buttermilk and combine with dry ingredients.

 Roll out onto lightly floured surface to ¼-inch thickness.

 Cut with biscuit cutter.

 Place on buttered baking pan and bake at 475 degrees for 10-12 minutes until golden brown.

SWEET POTATO BISCUITS

2	cups flour
1	teaspoon baking soda
1	teaspoon salt
⅓	cup shortening
1	tablespoon sugar
1	cup cooked, mashed sweet potatoes
¾	cup buttermilk

 Sift together flour, salt, baking soda and sugar.

 Cut in the shortening and add sweet potatoes.

 Stir in milk (more if necessary) to make stiff dough.

 Toss dough on floured board and knead lightly.

 Roll out to ½-inch thickness and cut with floured cutter.

 Bake at 450 degrees until golden brown.

Martha's Biscuits

This recipe was submitted by Mrs. W. D. Partee.

2   cups plain flour
2   teaspoons baking powder
1   teaspoon salt
⅛   teaspoon soda
3   tablespoons shortening
1   cup buttermilk

- Preheat oven to 475 degrees.
- Sift together flour, baking powder, soda and salt.
- Cut in shortening until mixture is almost like meal.
- Add buttermilk and knead mixture very lightly until mixed.
- Pour on a floured board and roll out.
- Cut biscuits.
- Bake for about 12 minutes.

Cornbread or Corn Muffins

Cornbread or corn muffins are a must with Southern meals and are especially good with soups and vegetables.

2   cups corn meal
1   egg
½   cup buttermilk
1   tablespoon granulated sugar
¼   cup butter or margarine

- Combine all ingredients in a mixing bowl.
- Mix with a whip. Do not beat.

176

- Pour into 12-15 muffin cups in muffin tins. If not using muffin cups, coat muffin pan with all-vegetable shortening.
- For cornbread, coat a baking pan with all-vegetable shortening and pour batter into pan.
- Bake at 350 degrees for 15-18 minutes until golden brown.
- Remove from oven and brush with melted butter.
- Cut cornbread into squares or remove muffins from tin.
- Serve hot.

BLUEBERRY MUFFINS

This recipe was submitted by the Hard Labor Creek
Blueberry Farm in Social Circle.

1	egg
½	cup milk
¼	cup salad oil
1 ½	cups all-purpose flour
½	cup granulated sugar
2	teaspoons baking powder
½	teaspoon salt
1	cup fresh blueberries, or ¾ cup drained frozen blueberries

- Mix all ingredients together.
- Pour into muffin cups.
- Bake at 400 degrees for 20-25 minutes.

UNFORGETTABLE!
---HAMBURG, GERMANY

177

BRAN MUFFINS

1	cup 100% bran flakes cereal
1	cup boiling water
½	cup shortening
3	eggs
1	cup sugar
¼	cup molasses
½	cup dark brown sugar
¼	cup honey
2 ½	cups all-purpose flour, sifted
2 ½	teaspoons baking soda
2	cups buttermilk
2	cups Kellogg's All-Bran cereal
1	cup raisins
1	cup chopped nuts, optional

- Pour 1 cup boiling water over 100% bran cereal and allow to cool.
- Cream the shortening, sugar, molasses and honey.
- Add eggs one at a time, beating after each addition.
- Add flour, soda, salt and buttermilk and mix well.
- Add cereal, raisins and nuts, if desired. Stir only until mixed well.
- Pour into lightly greased muffin tins or muffin cups.
- Bake at 400 degrees for 20 minutes.
- Batter will hold well in the refrigerator for 3-4 weeks in a closed container.

Yield: About 3 dozen.

SWEET POTATO BREAD

This recipe was submitted by Annette Taylor who is one of the fine cooks at the Blue Willow Inn Restaurant.

3	large sweet potatoes
4	tablespoons vanilla
1 ½	cups flour
4	eggs
2	tablespoons cinnamon
1 ½	teaspoons nutmeg
2	cups sugar
1	cup milk

- Wash and peel potatoes. Cover with water and boil until done.
- Drain water and mash potatoes.
- Add all other ingredients and mix well.
- Bake in a large loaf pan for 20-25 minutes at 350 degrees until done.
- If desired add pecans or walnuts and raisins or coconut.

SPINACH CORNBREAD

This recipe was submitted by Kitty Jacobs, Guidelines, Atlanta.

1	10-ounce package frozen chopped spinach
1	6-ounce package Martha White Mexican cornbread mix
½	teaspoon salt
½	cup melted margarine
¾	cup cottage cheese
1	cup chopped onions (cont. →)

179

4   large eggs, lightly beaten

 Thaw and drain spinach well, squeezing out moisture.
 Place in a mixing bowl and add all ingredients.
 Mix well and pour into a lightly greased 8-inch square baking dish.
 Bake at 400 degrees for 30 minutes or until lightly browned.

YEAST ROLLS

1   cup boiling water
¼   cup shortening
¼   cup butter
⅓   cup sugar
1   package active dry yeast
1   egg
1   teaspoon salt
3 ⅔   cups all-purpose flour

 In mixing bowl pour boiling water over butter and shortening.
 When shortening and butter have melted, add sugar and allow to cool until lukewarm.
 Add yeast and stir until dissolved.
 Add egg and salt.
 Sift flour into liquid, about ¾ cup at a time.
 Add enough flour to make a soft dough. Allow to rise and double, about an hour.
 Punch dough down and form into rolls and let it rise again until about doubled, about a half hour.
 Bake for 10 minutes at 350 degrees on ungreased baking pan. Brush with butter.
Yield: About 24 rolls

EXPERIENCING
SWEETS AND DESSERTS

*Guests at the Blue Willow Inn restuarant enjoy a variety
of desserts including hot cobbler and ice cream.*

181

Julian's Pecan Pie

This pie is a favorite of Louis's dad. During the holiday season, Julian bakes pecan pies for friends and neighbors and enjoys delivering his fresh pies on Thanksgiving and Christmas.

3	eggs, slightly beasten
½	cup light or dark corn syrup
½	cup pure maple syrup
½	cup granulated sugar
2½	tablespoons Mazola margarine, melted
1	cup pecans
1	teaspoon vanilla extract
1	teaspoon pure lemon extract
1	frozen pastry pie crust

- Preheat oven to 350 degrees.
- Combine all ingredients except pecans in a mixing bowl and stir until well blended.
- Add pecans and stir.
- Pour into thawed pie crust.
- Bake for 50-55 minutes.

Peanut Butter Pie

"A dixie meal without dessert? Unheard of! So is the number of to-drool-for sweet dishes on a table located so centrally you can't side step it with good intentions." Southern Living. There is always a fight over the last piece of peanut butter pie, but there is chocolate layer cake, lemon meringue pie, banana pudding, and whatever else our cooks decide on that day. One guest asked "Who made the Peanut Butter Pie? I want to marry her!"

1	8-ounce package cream cheese
1	cup 10x powdered sugar
¾-1	cup crunchy peanut butter
1	12-ounce carton Cool Whip
2	Graham Cracker Shells

182

- Mix cream cheese, sugar and peanut butter together.
- Fold in Cool Whip.
- Pour into pie shell and chill for several hours.
- Top with Cool Whip, serve and enjoy.

JULIAN'S SWEET POTATO PIE

*This pie is also a favorite of Louis's dad. This is good served warm or cold.
It's a must with Thanksgiving and Christmas dinners.*

2	**cups cooked, mashed sweet potatoes**
1	**cup granulated sugar**
¼	**cup butter or margarine, melted**
¼	**teaspoon salt**
1	**teaspoon vanilla extract**
1	**teaspoon pure lemon extract**
1	**14-ounce can Eagle Brand sweetened condensed milk**
2	**eggs**
1	**teaspoon ground cinnamon**
½	**teaspoon ground ginger**
1	**teaspoon ground nutmeg**
1	**9-inch frozen flaky pie crust**

- Preheat oven to 425 degrees.
- Combine all ingredients in a large mixing bowl and mix well.
- Pour into the frozen pie crust.
- Bake at 425 degrees for 15 minutes.
- Reduce heat to 350 degrees and bake for 35-40 minutes.
- If desired, garnish each slice with a small amount of whipped cream and nutmeg.

BUTTERMILK PIE

3	eggs, slightly beaten
1	cup sugar
2	tablespoons flour
½	cup melted butter
1	cup buttermilk
½	teaspoon vanilla
½	teaspoon lemon extract
1	unbaked 9-inch pastry pie shell

- In a mixing bowl combine eggs, sugar, flour and butter.
- Mix well.
- Add buttermilk, vanilla and lemon extract and mix.
- Pour into pie shell.
- Bake at 350 degrees for 45-50 minutes until pie is set and golden brown.

CHERRY CHEESE PIE

1	9-inch graham cracker pie shell
1	8-ounce package cream cheese, softened
1	14-ounce can Eagle Brand sweetened condensed milk
⅓	cup lemon juice, from concentrate
1	teaspoon vanilla extract
1	14-ounce can cherry pie filling, chilled

- In a large mixing bowl beat the cheese until fluffy.
- Gradually add condensed milk and beat until smooth.
- Stir in lemon juice and vanilla. (cont. →)

- Pour into graham cracker pie shell.
- Chill for 3 hours or until set.
- Top with cherry pie filling.
- Refrigerate and serve cold.

Serving Suggestion: Other toppings that can be used are ambrosia topping, glazed strawberry, blueberry and cranberry nut.

FRENCH SILK CHOCOLATE PIE

This recipe was given to Billie by Ruth Plympton, a special friend and fellow caterer.

1	**stick butter**
2	**squares semisweet chocolate**
2	**eggs**
¾	**cup sugar**
1	**teaspoon vanilla extract**
1	**8-inch baked pie shell**

- Cream butter and sugar until light and fluffy.
- Melt chocolate. Add to butter and sugar.
- Add vanilla and beat until smooth.
- Add eggs one at a time beating each 5 minutes.
- Pour into a baked pie shell.
- Refrigerate until set, about 3-4 hours.
- Top with whipped cream.
- Serve cold.

Egg Custard Pie

3   eggs, beaten
1   stick melted butter
¼   cup buttermilk
1¼   cups sugar
2   tablespoons flour
        pinch of salt

- Combine flour and sugar and mix well.
- Add the beaten eggs and butter.
- Mix.
- Add buttermilk and pinch of salt.
- Pour into an unbaked pastry pie shell and bake at 350 degrees for 20-25 minutes until done.

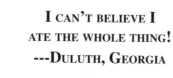

I can't believe I ate the whole thing!
---Duluth, Georgia

Coconut Cream Pie

1	cup granulated sugar
½	cup all-purpose flour
¼	teaspoon salt
3	cups milk
4	eggs
3	tablespoons butter
1½	teaspoons vanilla extract
1⅓	flaked coconut

- In saucepan combine sugar, flour and salt.
- Gradually stir in milk.
- Cook and stir the mixture until thickened and bubbly.
- Reduce heat.
- Cook and stir two more minutes and remove from heat.
- Separate egg yolks from whites and set aside whites.
- Beat egg yolks slightly.
- Slowly stir in 1 cup of hot mixture into yolks.
- Return egg mixture to saucepan and bring to slow boil.
- Cook and stir 2 more minutes.
- Remove from heat and stir in butter, vanilla flavoring and one cup of coconut.
- Pour hot mixture into baked pastry pie shell.
- Toast remaining coconut.
- Make meringue from egg whites.
- Spoon meringue over pie and sprinkle toasted coconut on top.
- Refrigerate and serve cool.

COCONUT PIE

This recipe was submitted by Patty Harrison from
Social Circle, Georgia.

2	**pastry pie shells**
½	**pound butter**
2	**cups shredded coconut**
2	**teaspoons vanilla**
6	**eggs**
3	**cups sugar**
½	**cup buttermilk**
2	**tablespoons flour**

🍴 Mix all ingredients.

🍴 Pour into two unbaked pastry pie shells.

🍴 Bake at 300 degrees until brown.

Yield: 2 pies

FRENCH COCONUT PIE

1½	**cups sugar**
1	**level tablespoon flour**
3	**eggs, beaten**
1	**stick soft butter**
¼	**cup buttermilk**
1	**cup flaked coconut**

🍴 Combine flour and sugar and mix well.

🍴 Add beaten eggs and mix.

🍴 Add other ingredients and mix well.

🍴 Pour into unbaked 9-inch pastry pie shell.

🍴 Bake at 350 degrees for 20-25 minutes until done.

LEMON MERINGUE PIE

1⅓	cups granulated sugar
1¾	cups cold water
½	cup cornstarch
⅛	teaspoon salt
4	egg yolks
3	tablespoons butter
2	tablespoons grated lemon rind
¼	cup lemon juice
1	9-inch pastry pie shell

- In a heavy saucepan combine granulated sugar, cornstarch and salt.
- Gradually add water, stirring until smooth.
- Cook over medium heat, stirring continuously, until mixture thickens and boils.
- Boil one minute, stirring continuously.
- Remove from heat.
- Beat egg yolks at high speed in mixture until thick.
- Gradually stir one-third of hot mixture into egg yolks.
- Add to remaining hot mixture stirring continuously.
- Return to heat and cook 2-3 minutes while stirring.
- Remove from heat.
- Add butter, lemon juice, and lemon rind.
- Stir to mix.
- Pour hot filling into 9-inch baked pastry pie shell.
- Top with meringue (recipe follows) and bake at 350 degrees for 12-14 minutes until meringue is browned.
- Let cool.

Meringue

⅓   **cup powdered sugar**
½   **teaspoon cream of tartar**
      egg whites of 4 eggs

- Sift powdered sugar.
- Allow the egg whites to come to room temperature.
- Combine egg whites and cream of tartar in a mixing bowl and beat at high speed with electric mixer until meringue is light and fluffy, about 3-4 minutes.

Pumpkin Pie

Good served with whipped topping.

1   **cup canned pumpkin pie mix**
1   **cup granulated sugar**
½   **cup butter**
½   **cup milk**
½   **teaspoon cinnamon**
1   **teaspoon vanilla flavoring**
1   **pastry pie crust**

- Combine all ingredients and mix well.
- Pour into unbaked 9-inch pie shell.
- Bake at 350 degrees for 30 minutes.
- Serve warm or cold.

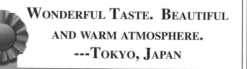

> **Wonderful Taste. Beautiful and warm atmosphere.**
> **---Tokyo, Japan**

FRIED PIE

This recipe was submitted by Ann Lowe, head cook at the Blue Willow Inn, and the Blue Willow Inn's first employee.

1	**bag dried peaches**
1	**cup sugar**
2	**cups water**
1	**cup flour**
2	**cups cooking oil**
6	**biscuits, from canned biscuits, uncooked**

In saucepan combine peaches, sugar and water.

Cook on low heat until peaches are tender. Drain peaches.

On lightly floured surface roll out each biscuit into thin sheets.

Fill each sheet on one side only with peaches.

Fold other side over and seal with a fork.

Dredge in flour.

Place in hot oil in large skillet and cook each side until brown, turning twice.

Drain on paper bags.

NOTE: When drained on paper towels, the pies have a tendency to stick to the towels. For Fried Pies with apple filling substitute dried apples for the peaches. Follow the same directions but add ½ teaspoon of cinnamon and ½ teaspoon of spice.

APPLE PIE

1	14-ounce can sliced apples
	or
1½	cups cooked apples
¼	cup light brown sugar
½	cup granulated sugar
2	tablespoons flour
¼	teaspoon salt
½	teaspoon cinnamon
¼	teaspoon nutmeg
2	tablespoons melted butter

- In mixing bowl combine all ingredients.
- Line bottom and sides of 9-inch pie plate with flaky pie crust. The crust should be slightly over the sides of the pie pan.
- Pour apples into pie shell.
- Top with flaky pie crust.
- Use fork to seal edges.
- Cut 3 or 4 , 1½-inch slits in pie.
- Baste with butter.
- Cook at 425 degrees for 40-45 minutes until golden brown.

PASTRY PIE CRUST

2¼	cups flour
1	teaspoon salt
⅔	cup all-vegetable shortening
⅓	cup ice cold water

- Mix flour, salt and shortening to a coarse mixture.
- Add water and mix.
- Divide dough and roll on floured surface.
- Place one crust in bottom of pie shell with crust slightly over the side of the shell.
- Place second crust on top of the pie.

PINEAPPLE UPSIDE-DOWN CAKE

1   **28-ounce box yellow cake mix**
1   **can pineapple rings (drain and reserve juice)**
      pineapple juice
      cherries without stems
      glaze (See recipe below)

      GLAZE:
1   **cup pineapple juice**
$\frac{1}{4}$ **cup butter**
$\frac{1}{2}$ **cup light brown sugar**

- Follow directions on cake mix except substitute pineapple juice for water.
- Combine butter, brown sugar and pineapple juice in sauce pan and bring to a boil.
- Layer bottom of lightly greased baking pan with pine apple rings and place a cherry in the center of each ring.
- Pour glaze over pineapples.
- Pour cake mix evenly over pineapple rings.
- Bake at 350 degrees for 35 minutes or until done with cake test. (cont. →)

-  After removing from oven, cover baking pan with larger pan.
-  Carefully turn cake upside down into larger tray and gently remove cake from pan.

Poppy Seed Cake

This recipe was submitted by Estelle Brandt from Chicago, Illinois.

2	**cups sugar**
1½	**cups Wesson oil**
3	**large eggs**
3	**cups sifted flour**
1½	**teaspoons baking soda**
1	**can Milnot**
1	**10-ounce can Solo poppy seeds**
1	**teaspoon vanilla extract**
1	**teaspoon ReaLemon concentrate lemon juice**

-  Combine sugar and Wesson oil. Beat to mix well.
-  Beat well after each egg.
-  Add Milnot, poppy seeds, vanilla and lemon and mix well.
-  Bake in 10-inch tube pan for 1 hour at 350 degrees.
-  Test with toothpick.

Frosting for Poppy Seed Cake

3	**ounces cream cheese**
2½	**cups sifted powdered sugar**
1	**teaspoon lemon juice from concentrate**

-  Allow cream cheese to come to room temperature.

194

- Place all ingredients in blender and mix well or mix with hand mixer.
- Spread over cooled cake.

OREO COOKIE CAKE
This dessert is also called Dirt Cake.

2   **12-ounce packages Cool Whip**
1   **large package Oreo cookies**
1   **16-ounce can cherry pie filling**

- In a clear glass bowl cover bottom with Cool Whip.
- Break cookies into crumbs.
- Add Oreo cookie crumbs, then Cool Whip, then cherry pie filling.
- Next add another layer of Cool Whip, Oreo cookie crumbs and Cool Whip.
- Top with whole Oreo cookies.
- Refrigerate 2-3 hours to season and serve chilled.

ICE CREAM CAKE

This recipe was submitted by Kitty Jacobs who works for Guidelines, Atlanta, an Atlanta tour company. For several years Kitty has been bringing bus tours to the Blue Willow Inn to experience the "Old South." Kitty has become a real friend of the Blue Willow Inn Restaurant.

1   **angel food cake**
1   **3-ounce package strawberry Jello**
1   **3-ounce package lime Jello**
1   **3-ounce package orange Jello**
1   **16-ounce package frozen strawberries (cont. →)**

195

1	14-ounce can blueberries
1	12-ounce can mandarin oranges
½	gallon vanilla ice cream

- Divide cake into 3 equal parts.
- In separate bowls, pull apart cake sections into bite size pieces.
- Pour a package of Jello crystals into each bowl of cake, mixing well with your fingers.
- Using tube pan that can be removed, mold strawberry cake mixture evenly around pan.
- Spread strawberries over cake and smooth evenly one-third of the ice cream evenly over strawberries.
- Spread lime Jello cake evenly next and cover with one-third of ice cream.
- Spread orange Jello cake and mandarin oranges next and cover with remaining one-third ice cream.
- Freeze. Remove tube pan and slice.

PETRA'S POUND CAKE

Petra Broberg was a dear friend of Billie's. Petra was one of the first graduates of the Chicago School of Nursing in the early 1900s. While Petra was engaged to be married, her best friend became terminally ill. Before she died she asked Petra to raise her two small daughters; Petra agreed, but her beau flew from the alter at the prospect of a ready-made family. From that time on, Petra dedicated her life to taking care of people no one else wanted or could care for. Billie and Petra met while Billie was in the children's home in Savannah and Petra was director of the Fresh Air Home in Tybee Island, Georgia. At this time Petra took Billie "under her wings." As Billie grew up and started a family of her own several years passed before Billie and Petra were reunited while visiting the same church in Savannah. This time Billie took Petra under <u>her</u> wings and looked after her until Petra's death in 1987. During the last six years of her life Petra lived with Billie and Louis.

2	**sticks butter**
6	**eggs**
½	**teaspoon baking soda**
3	**cups sugar**
1	**cup sour cream**
3	**cups flour**
1	**teaspoon vanilla**

- Grease and flour tube pan.
- Preheat oven to 350 degrees.
- Cream butter. Whip until creamy.
- Add sugar slowly and beat well.
- Add eggs gradually, one at a time.
- Beat at least 1 minute between eggs.
- Add baking soda to sour cream and beat 1 minute.
- Add sour cream and beat 1 minute.
- Add flavoring.
- Bake for 45 minutes until light brown.
- Test to be sure the cake is done. A toothpick inserted in the center should come out clean.

NOTE: One of Petra's favorite hobbies was cooking. She had mastered this recipe and made one of the best pound cakes anywhere. One reason may have been that after pouring batter into the tube pan she would bang the pan on the counter to "eliminate air pockets" which often caused Louis to check on her to see if she was destroying the kitchen. When she served "her" pound cake, she would always say that it "just isn't right" and enjoyed everyone telling her, "Oh no, it's wonderful." We remember one occasion when a friend replied, "Petra, you know, it isn't quite right." Petra was devastated, and he had to quickly admit he was teasing her. Never again did anyone tease her when she said "It just isn't right!" All of us really miss Petra and her "just right" pound cakes.

POUND CAKE

This recipe was submitted by Patty Harrison.

2	cups sugar
1	cup Crisco shortening
4	eggs
1	cup sweet milk
2½	cups plain flour
½	cup self-rising flour
1	teaspoon vanilla flavoring

Mix sugar, Crisco and eggs.

Add flour and milk a little at a time, mixing continuously.

Add vanilla and mix.

Pour into a greased tube cake pan.

Bake at 350 degrees for 1 hour.

NOTE: Top will be moist.

FRESH APPLE CAKE

This is a favorite recipe of Elton and Jean Wright of Social Circle. Elton is one of the managers of the Blue Willow Inn and usually does the cooking at home.

2	cups sugar
½	cup Wesson oil
3	large eggs
3	cups all-purpose flour
1	teaspoon salt
1	teaspoon baking soda
1½	teaspoons vanilla extract

198

3   **cups peeled, diced, firm Granny Smith apples**
¾   **cup flaked coconuts**
1   **cup black walnut or pecan pieces**

- Mix sugar and oil.
- Add eggs and beat well.
- Combine flour, salt and baking soda and add to oil mixture.
- Stir in vanilla, apples, coconut and nuts.
- Spoon into 9-inch greased pound cake or tube pan.
- Cook for 80-90 minutes at 325 degrees.
- Cool and serve.

Coco Lopez Coconut Cake

This recipe was submitted by Betty Henderson who makes this cake for Louis and Billie every Christmas. It is excellent and umh umh good!

1   **box yellow pudding cake mix**
1   **14-ounce can sweetened condensed milk**
1   **15-ounce can Coco Lopez cream of coconut**
1   **12-ounce package Cool Whip whipped topping**
1   **12-ounce package frozen flaked coconut**

- Follow the directions on cake mix and bake in 13x9-inch pan.
- When the cake comes out of oven immediately poke holes all over the cake with a fork.
- Pour sweetened condensed milk over cake.
- After the cake has cooled put cream of coconut over the cake. (cont. →)

 Spread Cool Whip over the cake and cover the cake with coconut.

NOTE: This cake is better if made a day ahead.

PINEAPPLE NUT CAKE

This recipe was submitted by Elaine Jones. This is an old recipe that originally called for flour, baking soda, sugar, etc. She modified it by using a cake mix to save time and money. However, she found that by using the new "Lite" cake mixes, you don't have to add oil or butter which is another time and money saver. If you don't have an available lite cake mix, you can use any yellow cake mix and follow directions on box except eliminate half a cup of the water required to allow for the juice of the pineapple.

1	box "Lite" yellow cake mix
1	14-ounce can crushed pineapple, with juice (do not drain)
¾	cup water
3	large eggs

 Combine above ingredients.

 Lightly grease 13x9-inch pan.

 Pour in batter and bake for 30 minutes at 350 degrees until golden brown and a toothpick inserted in the center comes out clean.

PINEAPPLE NUT CAKE ICING

¾	cup evaporated milk
1	stick real butter
1	cup sugar (cont. →)

1   **cup coconut**
1   **cup walnuts, chopped**

- Combine milk, butter and sugar in saucepan.
- Bring to boil over medium heat, stirring frequently.
- Cook for five minutes on medium heat.
- Turn off heat and stir in coconut and nuts.
- Pour over cake.

COCA-COLA CAKE

This recipe is from Jane and Michael Stern, the talented GOURMET *Magazine writers who featured the Blue Willow Inn in the April 14, 1995 edition of* GOURMET. *Use with Broiled Peanut Butter Frosting.*

2   **cups flour**
2   **cups sugar**
2   **sticks butter, melted**
2   **tablespoons unsweetened cocoa**
1   **cup Coca-Cola, with fizz**
½   **cup buttermilk**
2   **eggs, beaten**
1   **teaspoon baking soda**
1   **teaspoon vanilla extract**
1½   **cup miniature marshmallows**

- Preheat oven to 350 degrees.
- Grease and flour a 9x13x2-inch sheet cake pan.
- Combine flour and sugar in a large bowl.
- Combine melted butter, cocoa and Coca-Cola and pour over flour and sugar mixture.
- Stir until well blended.
- Add buttermilk, beaten eggs, soda and vanilla. (cont.→)

- Mix well.
- Stir in marshmallows.
- Pour into prepared pan.
- Bake for 40 minutes.
- Remove cake from oven and frost while still barely warm.
  NOTE: Use Broiled Peanut Butter Frosting.

BROILED PEANUT BUTTER FROSTING

6   **tablespoons butter**
1   **cup dark brown sugar**
⅔   **cup smooth peanut butter**
¼   **cup milk**
⅔   **cup chopped peanuts**

- Cream butter, sugar and peanut butter.
- Beat in milk.
- Fold in nuts.
- Spread over cake.
- Place the frosted cake under broiler about 4 inches from heat source.
- Broil just a few seconds, or until topping starts to bubble.
  NOTE: Watch constantly and be careful not to scorch frosting. Frost cake while it is barely warm.

CHOCOLATE POUND CAKE
This recipe was given to us by Petra Broberg.

2	sticks butter or margarine
½	cup shortening
3	cups sugar
3	cups all-purpose flour
1	teaspoon vanilla
½	teaspoon baking powder
¼	cup milk
¼	cup sour cream
½	cup powdered cocoa
5	eggs
½	teaspoon salt

- Preheat oven to 325 degrees.
- Cream butter, shortening and sugar.
- Add eggs one at a time. Beat for 1 minute after each egg.
- Sift dry ingredients 3 times. Add alternately with flour, milk and sour cream.
- Add vanilla and beat 1 minute.
- Pour into tube pan.
- Bake at 325 degrees for 1 hour.
- Turn oven down to 300 degrees and bake for 15 more minutes.
- Cool for 1 hour in the pan before removing from pan.

APPLE WALNUT CAKE

1⅔	cups sugar
2	eggs
½	cup vegetable oil
2	teaspoons vanilla extract
2	cups all-purpose flour
2	teaspoons baking soda
1 ½	teaspoons ground cinnamon
1	teaspoon salt
½	teaspoon ground nutmeg
4	cups chopped, unpeeled apples
1	cup chopped walnuts

- In a mixing bowl, beat the sugar and eggs.
- Add oil and vanilla, mix well.
- Combine flour, baking soda, cinnamon, salt and nutmeg.
- Gradually add to sugar mixture, mixing well.
- Stir in apples and walnuts.
- Pour into greased and floured 13x9x2-inch baking pan.
- Bake at 350 degrees for 50-55 minutes or until cake tests done.
- Cool on a wire rack.

FROSTING

2	3-ounce packages cream cheese, softened
3	tablespoons butter or margarine, softened
1	teaspoon vanilla extract
1½	cups confectioner's sugar

- Beat cream cheese, butter and vanilla in mixing bowl.

- ♨ Gradually add confectioner's sugar until frosting is light.
- ♨ Frost cake after cake is cooled.

Yield: 16-20 servings

PUNCH BOWL CAKE

This recipe was submitted by Keith Browning who has worked for Louis and Billie off and on at the restaurant and with catering since 1985. While attending a function away from the restaurant, Keith was served Punch Bowl Cake. The cake was a hit at the function, and Keith requested the recipe. We first served this on a Mother's Day, and it has become a favorite dessert for many of our customers.

1	**Duncan Hines yellow cake mix**
1	**16-ounce can cherry pie filling**
1	**16-ounce can crushed pineapple**
2	**16-ounce packages Cool Whip**
1	**12-ounce package shredded coconut**
½	**cup chopped pecans**

- ♨ Follow the directions on the cake mix and bake the cake.
- ♨ Once the cake has cooled, crumble one layer of the cake into a punch bowl along with half of the coconut.
- ♨ Spread the pineapple over the cake.
- ♨ Cover with one container of Cool Whip and top with one half of the pecans.
- ♨ Crumble the second layer of cake over the mixture.
- ♨ Spread the coconut then cherry pie filling on top.
- ♨ Top with the remaining Cool Whip and pecans.
- ♨ Refrigerate overnight.

STRAWBERRY CAKE

Billie makes this cake for their son Chip's birthday every year.
This is his favorite cake.

1	**package white cake mix**
1	**3-ounce package strawberry Jello**
⅔	**cup Wesson oil**
½	**cup water**
1	**cup frozen, drained strawberries**
4	**eggs**

- Sift the cake mix and Jello together. Add oil.
- Add eggs, one at a time. Mix, but do not beat.
- Blend in strawberries until they are somewhat shredded.
- Bake at 350 degrees for 30 minutes in greased and sugared cake pans or bake for 45 minutes in tube pan.
- Cover top and sides with strawberry icing.

STRAWBERRY CAKE ICING

1	**16-ounce package confectioner's sugar**
1	**stick butter or margarine at room temperature**
1	**teaspoon vanilla**
¼	**cup sliced fresh or frozen strawberries**
	milk or cream

- Combine all ingredients in mixing bowl or food processor.
- Mix well at medium speed until light and fluffy.
- Add milk or cream as needed for fluffy texture.

CHOCOLATE-CHERRY CAKE

This recipe was submitted by Nellie Baines who is one of the head waitresses at the Blue Willow Inn Restaurant. Several times a year Nell bakes her Chocolate-Cherry Cake for employees, and there is never a crumb left. Nell always seems to have the energy to do for others--she is always baking sweets to give to someone at the restaurant or to take to patients in the nursing home.

1	**can cherry pie filling**
1	**package fudge cake mix**
1	**teaspoon almond extract**
2	**eggs, beaten**

- Drain cherry pie filling into mixing bowl.
- Set aside cherries.
- Add the cake mix, almond extract and eggs to drained liquid.
- Mix well.
- Fold in cherries.
- Pour into greased and floured 9x13-inch baking pan or casserole dish.
- Bake at 350 degrees for 30-35 minutes.

FROSTING

1	**cup granulated sugar**
5	**tablespoons butter**
½	**cup milk**
1	**teaspoon almond extract**
1	**6-ounce package semisweet chocolate chips**

- In small saucepan combine sugar, butter and milk.

(cont. →)

- Bring to a boil and boil for one minute, stirring constantly.
- Remove from heat and add almond extract and chocolate chips.
- Beat with mixer until smooth.
- Cool and spread over cake.

BLUEBERRY BANANA PECAN NUT CAKE

At the Blue Willow Inn Restaurant we slice the cake and serve it on a large platter with blueberry sauce in a small bowl in the middle. Guests can serve themselves with cake and sauce on top. This is a wonderful brunch item.

1	**cup blueberries**
12	**ounces butter, softened**
1½	**cups sugar**
4	**eggs**
3	**large ripe mashed bananas**
1	**14-ounce package of sour cream**
2	**cups all-purpose flour**
1	**teaspoon baking soda**
1	**teaspoon baking powder**
¼	**teaspoon salt**
1	**cup chopped pecans**

- Rinse and drain fresh blueberries.
- Cream the butter and sugar.
- Add eggs one at a time, mixing well.
- Add bananas and sour cream.
- Mix well.
- Add dry ingredients. (cont. →)

- Fold blueberries and pecans into batter. If using frozen blueberries, dust with small amount of flour.
- Pour batter into 2 greased and floured 9x5x2-inch loaf pans.
- Bake at 375 degrees for 45-55 minutes or until a tooth pick inserted in the center comes out clean.
- Cool.

Serving Suggestion: Top with warm blueberry sauce im mediately before serving.

Yield: 24 servings

PEANUT BUTTER CAKE

½	**cup shortening**
1	**cup peanut butter**
1½	**cups sugar**
2	**cups plain flour**
1	**teaspoon baking soda**
1½	**cups buttermilk**
1	**teaspoon vanilla extract**
3	**eggs**

- Cream shortening, peanut butter and sugar.
- Add eggs one at a time, beating after each addition.
- Add soda to flour and add alternately with buttermilk to mixture.
- Add vanilla flavoring.
- Mix well.
- Pour into 3 large greased and sugared layer pans and bake at 350 degrees for 30 minutes.

Peanut Butter Cake Frosting

1   **stick butter, softened**
1   **16-ounce package confectioner's sugar**
1   **cup peanut butter**
½   **teaspoon vanilla extract**
       milk, as needed to cream above ingredients

- Mix all ingredients together.
- Add small amount of milk or cream to make frosting creamy for spreading on cake.

Chocolate Cookie Sheet Cake

Pat Whitley of Monroe, Georgia, gave us this recipe several years ago. It has been one of the favorite desserts at the Blue Willow Inn. Frost with Chocolate Cookie Sheet Cake Icing.

2   **cups plain flour**
2   **cups sugar**
½   **teaspoon salt**
2   **sticks margarine, melted**
1   **cup water**
3   **tablespoons cocoa**
2   **eggs, well beaten**
1   **teaspoon baking soda**
½   **cup buttermilk**
1   **teaspoon vanilla extract**

- Sift the flour; measure and resift with sugar and salt.
- In saucepan combine margarine, water and cocoa.
- Bring to a boil and pour over flour and sugar mixture.

210

- In another bowl combine beaten eggs, baking soda, buttermilk and vanilla.
- Beat well.
- Add to first mixture and mix well.
- Bake in a greased and floured shallow pan at 350 degrees for 20 minutes.
- Make Chocolate Cookie Sheet Cake icing while this is cooking.

Chocolate Cookie Sheet Cake Icing

Use with Chocolate Cookie Sheet Cake. Make icing last five minutes cake is baking.

1	**stick butter, melted**
3	**tablespoons cocoa**
7	**tablespoons milk**
1	**16-ounce package confectioner's sugar**
1	**tablespoon vanilla extract**
1	**cup chopped pecans**

- During the last five minutes cake is baking, mix butter, cocoa and milk in saucepan.
- Heat over low heat.
- Do not boil.
- Remove from heat and gradually add pecans, sugar and vanilla.
- Pour over cake as soon as it is removed from the oven.
  NOTE: For best results, double icing recipe.

Eight Layer Chocolate Cake

This recipe was submitted by Seena Wilkes from Surrency, Georgia. She makes this cake for her family and friends on birthdays and other special occasions.

1   **box Duncan Hines butter recipe cake mix. (Must be butter recipe cake mix.) Baker's Joy spray**

- Follow directions on Duncan Hines butter cake mix box.
- After mixing, spray eight, 8-inch cake pans with Baker's Joy spray and divide the mixture equally among the 8 pans.
- Cook four pans at a time at 350 degrees until golden brown.

For Icing

2	**cups sugar**
½	**cup canned evaporated milk**
½	**teaspoon vanilla**
⅓	**cup cocoa**
2	**sticks margarine**
5	**marshmallows**

- Mix 2 sticks of margarine in pot.
- Mix together sugar, milk and cocoa
- Boil for 2 minutes.
- Remove from heat and add ½ teaspoon vanilla and 5 marshmallows.
- Beat it until creamy enough to spread.
- Spread icing on each of the eight layers of cake as you stack them on top of each other.

ORANGE COCONUT CAKE

This recipe was submitted by Patty Harrison.

1	box Duncan Hines Orange Supreme Cake mix
1	3-ounce package orange flavored Jello
1	cup water
⅓	cup vegetable oil
2	eggs
1	teaspoon orange flavoring
1	cup mandarin orange slices
1	16-ounce package sour cream
¼	cup frozen orange juice
1	12-ounce package frozen shredded coconut
2	cups sugar
1	teaspoon orange flavoring
1	8-ounce package Cool Whip

- Combine cake mix, Jello mix, water, ⅓ cup oil, 2 eggs and 1 teaspoon orange flavoring.
- Pour batter into 4 prepared 8-inch pans and bake according to directions on cake box.
- For filling, combine sour cream, orange juice, coconut, sugar and 1 teaspoon orange flavoring.
- Mix well.
- Reserve 1 cup of filling for frosting.
- Spread remaining filling between layers.
- For frosting fold Cool Whip into reserved filling.
- Spread on top and sides of cake.
- Decorate with mandarin oranges.
- Refrigerate overnight.

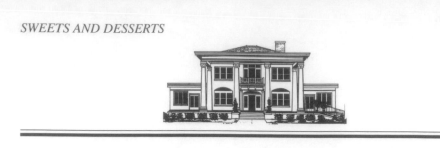

Orange Coconut Cake

This recipe was submitted by Shirley C. Wood. Mrs. Wood's husband is the minister of the First Baptist Church in Social Circle. Both she and her husband are frequent guests at the Blue Willow Inn Restaurant. When we asked for a recipe for the cookbook, Mrs. Wood shared with us a recipe that has been in her family for three generations. Her grandmother cooked the Orange Coconut Cake for every Christmas dinner. Her mother then cooked the same recipe for Christmas dinners at her home. Shirley Wood now cooks the traditional Orange Coconut Cake recipe every year at Christmas. Mrs. Wood's grandmother originally copied the recipe from the 1908 edition of "Rumford Complete Cookbook." The recipe is so old that no cooking temperature is noted. The recipes in the book called for cooking in either a moderate oven or a hot oven.

2	**cups sugar**
1	**cup butter**
3	**egg whites**
5	**egg yolks**
⅓	**level teaspoon salt**
2	**cups flour**
½	**cup water**
1½	**level teaspoon Rumford baking powder**
	juice and grated rind of orange

- Beat butter and sugar to cream.
- Add yolks of eggs and water, then the juice and rind of the orange.
- Add the flour, salt and baking powder, sifted together.
- Fold in very gently the stiffly beaten egg whites.
- Bake for 20 minutes in hot oven in large layer cake pans.
- Put the layers together with orange-coconut filling.

ORANGE-COCONUT FILLING

1	egg
1	cup grated coconut
1	cup whipped cream
½	cup powdered sugar
	juice of one orange
	grated rind of one orange

- Beat the eggs until light.
- Add whipped cream and sugar.
- Add orange rind, coconut and orange juice.
- Spread between layers and on top of cake.

CHOCOLATE MACAROONS

This recipe was submitted by Nancy East who was given this recipe at a U.S. Marine Corps Officer's Wives coffee in Norfolk, Virginia in 1965. This is the first time she has shared this recipe. Nancy is the head hostess at the Blue Willow Inn Restaurant and not only do the customers love Nancy, but she loves the customers. She is the perfect example of Southern hospitality.

4	egg whites
1	cup granulated sugar
½	teaspoon salt
2	teaspoons vanilla extract
12	ounces semisweet chocolate bits (must be real chocolate)
2⅔	cups shredded coconuts

- Beat egg whites until stiff. (cont. →)

- Slowly add the sugar, salt and vanilla while beating.
- Melt chocolate bits.
- Fold in chocolate and coconut into mixture.
- Drop by rounded teaspoonfuls onto lightly greased cookie sheets.
- Bake at 350 degrees for 10-15 minutes.
  Yield: about 4 dozen

WHITE CHOCOLATE MACADAMIA NUT COOKIES

This recipe was submitted by Sandra Conner who loves cookies of all kinds. The restaurant often sends Sandra and her staff oatmeal and chocolate chip cookies. She has been Louis and Billie's banker for several years. When times were "lean" Sandra always encouraged them by saying, "Hang in there. You're going to make it. I have faith in you," and she is appreciated and loved more than she can imagine.

½	**cup butter**
½	**cup shortening**
¾	**cup packed brown sugar**
½	**cup sugar**
1	**large egg**
1½	**teaspoons vanilla**
2	**cups all-purpose flour**
1	**teaspoon baking soda**
6	**ounces white chocolate chips**
7	**ounces macadamia nuts**

- In a mixing bowl, combine all ingredients and mix well.
- Spoon onto a lightly greased baking pan.
- Bake at 350 degrees for 8-10 minutes.
  NOTE: It's a good idea to double this recipe, as these go fast!

216

CHEWY OATMEAL COOKIES

¾	cup butter flavored Crisco shortening
1¼	cups firmly packed light brown sugar
1	egg
⅓	cup milk
1½	teaspoons vanilla flavoring
3	cups Quaker Oaks, quick or old-fashioned, un-cooked
1	cup all-purpose flour
½	teaspoon baking soda
½	teaspoon salt
¼	teaspoon cinnamon
1	cup raisins
1	cup coarsely chopped walnuts

- Heat oven to 375 degrees.
- Lightly grease the baking sheet with small amount of butter flavored Crisco.
- Combine Crisco, brown sugar, egg, milk and vanilla in a large bowl.
- Beat at medium speed until well blended.
- Combine oats, flour, baking soda, salt and cinnamon.
- Mix into creamed mixture at low speed until blended.
- Stir in raisins and nuts.
- Drop rounded tablespoons of dough 2 inches apart on greased baking sheet.
- Bake for 10-12 minutes or until lightly browned.

Yield: 2 ½ dozen cookies

CHOCOLATE OATMEAL COOKIES
This recipe was submitted by Kim Partain.

1	stick butter
2	cups sugar
½	cup peanut butter
4	tablespoons cocoa
4	cups oatmeal
½	cup pecans

- In saucepan over medium heat, melt butter.
- Add cocoa and sugar.
- Bring to a boil and boil for 3 minutes.
- Add peanut butter until well blended.
- Add oatmeal and stir well.
- Add pecans and mix.
- Drop by teaspoon onto waxed paper and let cool.

MELANIE'S CHOCOLATE CHIP COOKIES
This recipe was submitted by Melanie Jackson, our Catering and Marketing Director. It was given to her by her stepmother and comes all the way from Missouri.

2¼	cups all-purpose flour
1	teaspoon baking soda
1	teaspoon salt
2	eggs
2	sticks butter, melted
¾	cup firmly packed brown sugar
¼	cup granulated sugar
1	package vanilla instant pudding
1	teaspoon vanilla
1	12-ounce package of semi-sweet chocolate chips chopped pecans, optional

Reese's Pieces, optional

- Combine flour, soda, and salt in bowl and set aside.
- In separate bowl, combine eggs and butter. Mix with electric mixer until creamy.
- Add sugars, vanilla and instant vanilla pudding and mix well.
- Slowly add flour mixture.
- After all is well mixed, fold in chocolate chips.
- Drop by heaping teaspoons onto an ungreased cookie sheet 3 inches apart.
- Bake at 375 degrees for 8 to 10 minutes on center rack of oven.

BLUE WILLOW SQUARES

These are sometimes called Park Avenue Squares.

1	**18-ounce package of yellow cake mix**
¼	**pound butter or margarine softened**
1	**cup pecans, chopped**
1	**8-ounce block softened Philadelphia Cream Cheese**
1	**16-ounce package confectioner's sugar**
3	**eggs**

- Mix by hand with a spoon the butter, yellow cake mix, chopped pecans and one egg.
- Mix well.
- Press by hand into an ungreased 8x11-inch baking pan. Use ice water to chill your hands for easier handling.
- Combine the softened cream cheese and 2 slightly beaten eggs. Add powdered sugar and mix. Mixture should be slightly lumpy.
- Spoon over cake mixture and spread evenly. (cont.→)

■ Bake at 350 degrees for 35-40 minutes until golden brown.

■ Cool one hour and cut into squares.

FROZEN LEMON SQUARES

¼   **cup butter or margarine**
1¼   **cups graham cracker crumbs**
¼   **cup sugar**
3   **egg yolks**
1   **14-ounce can sweetened condensed milk**
½   **cup lemon juice, from concentrate**
       whipped topping

■ Combine margarine, graham cracker crumbs and sugar.

■ Press in bottom of 8 or 9-inch square pan.

■ In a medium bowl, beat egg yokes. Stir in sweetened condensed milk then lemon juice.

■ Pour into a prepared crust.

■ Top with whipped topping.

■ Freeze for 4-6 hours or until firm.

■ Let stand for 10 minutes before cutting.

■ Garnish with lemon peel.

Yield: 9 servings

CHEWIES

¼   **pound butter, or margarine**
1   **pound light brown sugar**
2   **cups self-rising flour**

3   **eggs (chicken eggs work best)**
2   **cups pecans or walnuts, chopped**
1   **teaspoon vanilla flavoring**

- Melt butter.
- Add sugar.
- Stir for 10 minutes. Do not overstir or understir.
- Add the eggs, one at a time and beat well after adding each egg.
- Blend in flour and vanilla and beat well.
- Add nuts and mix.
- Bake in 9x13-inch pan for 30-45 minutes until brown at 325 degrees.

ALICE'S BROWNIES

The children's grandmother always prepared this special treat at Christmas. After Alice passed on, this tradition was continued by our son Chip, as Christmas just wouldn't have been the same without them.

1½   **sticks butter or margarine**
4   **eggs**
1   **teaspoon vanilla flavoring**
1½   **cups self-rising flour**
2   **cups sugar**
1½   **ounces unsweetened chocolate**
2½   **cups pecans**

- Melt butter and chocolate together.
- Beat eggs.
- Add sugar and mix well.
- Add flour and mix well. (cont.→)

- Add vanilla and mix well.
- Add pecans and mix well.
- Pour into 9x13-inch greased pan.
- Bake at 325 degrees for 20-30 minutes.

ICING FOR ALICE'S BROWNIES

1	ounce butter (approximately ½-inch of stick)
½	ounce unsweetened chocolate
1	teaspoon vanilla flavoring
8	ounces 10X powdered sugar (½ box)
1	teaspoon instant Maxwell House coffee
½	cup water

- Melt butter and chocolate.
- Add vanilla, coffee and water together.
- Mix.
- Add spoonful by spoonful to sugar mixture until smooth.
- Spread over hot brownies.

LOUIS'S BROWNIES

These are great chewy brownies (especially for large groups).

2	packages brownie mix, Pillsbury or Duncan Hines, 26 or 28-ounce size
¾	cup chocolate icing
1	cup chopped pecans
¼	cup granulated sugar
	all vegetable shortening
	water
	liquid vegetable oil
	eggs

- Follow the directions on packaged brownie mix EXCEPT use one less egg than called for in recipe and use ½ cup less oil.
- Add all ingredients together.
- Mix gently. Do not beat.
- Grease ½ sheet pan with shortening and coat with granulated sugar.
- Pour and spread mix on sheet pans.
- Bake at 350 degrees for 15-17 minutes.

  NOTE: Remove from oven while center of pans are still loose. If this recipe is cooked until center of pans are firm, the end result will be hard and crisp brownies which are overcooked. Be careful.

  Yield: 75-85 brownies.

DONNA'S FUDGE

This recipe was submitted by Billie's daughter, Donna Sanders and is one of Louis's favorites. At his request, Donna makes him a tin of fudge at Christmas, Father's Day and on his birthday.

1	**16-ounce package confectioner's sugar**
½	**cup powdered cocoa**
¼	**cup milk**
1	**teaspoon vanilla extract**
1	**stick butter, softened**
1	**cup pecans or walnuts, chopped (optional)**

- Melt margarine in medium saucepan.
- Add remaining ingredients and stir until completely dissolved.
- Pour into an ungreased 9x9-inch pan.
- Cool, cut and enjoy!

223

BLUEBERRY COBBLER

*This recipe was submitted by The Hard Labor Creek
Blueberry Farm in Social Circle.*

1   **cup self-rising flour**
1   **cup granulated sugar**
1   **cup milk**
1   **stick butter, or margarine melted**
2   **cups blueberries**

- Mix all ingredients except blueberries.
- Place blueberries in baking dish.
- Pour mixture over blueberries.
- Bake at 375 degrees for 35 minutes.

PEACH COBBLER

*Peach Cobbler is served almost every day at the Blue Willow Inn. Our
customers would not let us open the doors without it. Try it with vanilla ice
cream or whipped cream.*

1   **28-ounce can sliced peaches**
1   **cup granulated sugar**
1   **cup self-rising flour**
½   **cup melted butter, divided**

- Coarsely mix one cup sugar, flour and ¼ cup of butter together.
- On bottom of baking dish sprinkle ⅓ of mixture.
- Add peaches.

- Top peaches with remaining butter and sugar (reserve 2 tablespoons of sugar and 1 ounce of butter).
- Top peaches with remainder of flour mixture.
- Sprinkle top with remainder of sugar and butter.
- Bake at 350 degrees for 30-40 minutes until brown and bubbly. Serve hot.

NOTE: When using fresh peaches, peel and slice peaches. Sprinkle with an additional ½ cup of sugar and refrigerate for 2-3 hours.

HOT APPLE CRISP

Great with vanilla ice cream.

1	**16-ounce can apple pie filling**
1	**cup light brown sugar, divided**
½	**cup granulated sugar**
¼	**cup water**
1	**tablespoon lemon juice**
¼	**teaspoon cinnamon**
¼	**teaspoon nutmeg**
¼	**teaspoon apple pie spice**
¾	**cup self-rising flour**
⅓	**cup melted butter, divided**

- In a mixing bowl, combine flour, ½ cup light brown sugar, ¼ cup granulated sugar and ¼ cup of butter.
- Mix until coarse.
- Sprinkle half of the mixture on the bottom of a 13x9x2-inch casserole dish or baking pan. (cont.→)

- Add apple pie filling and gently spread evenly over pan.
- Sprinkle the water, lemon juice and spices over apples.
- Cover with the balance of the granulated sugar and ¼ cup of brown sugar.
- Cover with rest of flour mixture and top with remaining brown sugar, granulated sugar and butter.
- Cook at 350 degrees for 45-50 minutes until golden brown and bubbly.

APPLE BROWN BETTY

6	**peeled, cored, sliced tart apples**
1½	**cups graham cracker crumbs**
½	**cup water**
½	**cup molasses**
¼	**cup brown sugar**
½	**cup melted butter**
½	**teaspoon cinnamon**

- Sprinkle half of the cracker crumbs in the bottom of a baking dish.
- Place ½ of the sliced apples on top of the crumbs.
- Repeat layers.
- Mix the water, molasses, brown sugar and butter.
- Add cinnamon and mix.
- Pour over top of cracker crumbs.
- Bake at 350 degrees covered for 40 minutes.
- Uncover and bake an additional 15 minutes.
- Serve hot.

BANANA NUT BREAD

½   cup shortening
1   cup sugar
2   eggs
1   cup overripe mashed bananas
1   cup chopped pecans
2   cups sifted all-purpose flour
3   teaspoons baking powder
1   teaspoon lemon juice
½   teaspoon salt

 Cream shortening and sugar together.

 Beat the eggs until light and add lemon juice.

 Blend with creamed mixture.

 Sift flour, baking powder and salt together and mix quickly into banana mixture.

 Add nuts.

 Bake in a greased loaf pan at 350 degrees for 1¼ hours or until a toothpick inserted in the middle comes out clean.

GINGERBREAD

Good served with Lemon Sauce.

¾   cup brown sugar
¾   cup molasses
¾   cup melted butter
2   eggs, well beaten
2½   cups plain flour

½   teaspoon baking powder
½   teaspoon salt
2   teaspoons soda
2½   teaspoons ground ginger
1½   teaspoons cinnamon
⅓   teaspoon cloves
1   cup boiling water

- In a mixing bowl mix sugar, molasses and butter.
- Add eggs.
- Sift together the flour and all other dry ingredients into bowl and mix well.
- Add boiling water and mix well.
- Bake in 9x13x2-inch floured pan for 35-40 minutes until tested done with a wooden pick.
- Cool.

BANANA PUDDING

2   eggs, beaten
6   tablespoons flour
4   cups milk
1   teaspoon vanilla
9   ounces whipped topping
8   tablespoons sugar
4-5   bananas
        vanilla wafer cookies
        dash salt

- In a saucepan combine flour, sugar, salt and eggs.
- Add milk a little at a time and stir until smooth.

- Cook over medium heat until thickened, stirring continuously.
- Cool thoroughly.
- Line the bottom of a casserole dish with vanilla wafers, then bananas.
- Repeat until dish is ⅔ full.
- Cover with pudding.
- Cool.
- Top with whipped topping.
- Refrigerate leftover pudding.

RICE PUDDING

4	**cups cooked rice**
1½	**cups sugar**
4	**cups milk**
1	**cup raisins**
½	**teaspoon nutmeg**
4	**eggs, slightly beaten**
	dash salt

- In a mixing bowl combine all ingredients and mix well.
- Bake in casserole dish at 350 degrees for 1½ hours until brown.
- Serve hot.

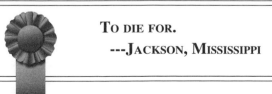

TO DIE FOR.

---JACKSON, MISSISSIPPI

229

BREAD PUDDING

Good with Lemon Sauce or Whiskey Sauce.

8-10	**leftover biscuits**
	OR
½	**loaf toasted white bread**
4	**eggs**
1¾	**cups sugar**
¼	**cup vanilla**
1	**teaspoon cinnamon**
1	**teaspoon nutmeg**
1	**quart milk**
1	**stick butter, softened**
¾	**cup raisins**

- In a large mixing bowl beat eggs until frothy.
- Add sugar, vanilla, cinnamon and nutmeg and beat well.
- Add butter and milk and mix well.
- Coarsely crumble biscuits or bread and add to mixture.
- Mix well. Do not beat.
- Pour mixture into an ungreased 13x9x2-inch pan.
- Bake in a 350 degree oven for 40-45 minutes until brown.
- Serve warm.

BLUEBERRY DESSERT

*This recipe was submitted by The Hard Labor Creek
Blueberry Farm in Social Circle.*

1	cup all-purpose flour
1	stick butter, softened
¼	cup dark brown sugar
1	cup chopped pecans
1	8-ounce package cream cheese, softened
1	8-ounce package Cool Whip
1	cup sugar, divided
1	teaspoon vanilla extract
1	quart blueberries
2	heaping teaspoons cornstarch

- Combine flour, butter, dark brown sugar and pecans.
- Mix well.
- Press into bottom of 9x2x13-inch baking dish.
- Cook for15-20 minutes at 350 degrees until slightly brown.
- Mix together cream cheese, Cool Whip, ¾ cup sugar and vanilla.
- Spread over cooled base.
- In saucepan combine blueberries, cornstarch and ¼ cup sugar.
- Cook over medium heat stirring often until thickened.
- Cool and spread over cream cheese layer.
- Refrigerate until served.

Strawberry Candies

1	14-ounce can sweetened condensed milk
1	pound finely ground coconut
2	3-ounce packages of strawberry Jello, divided
1	cup almonds, finely ground
1	tablespoon sugar
1	teaspoon vanilla flavoring
1	4-ounce can decorator icing

- Combine milk, coconut, ⅔ Jello, almonds, sugar and vanilla.
- Shape into strawberries.
- Roll candies in remaining Jello, coating thoroughly.
- Let dry until firm.
- Make leaves with icing.
- Store refrigerated in covered container .

  NOTE: Old recipe called for green sugar (sugar with green food coloring) instead of canned icing.

  Yield: about 48 large strawberries

Strawberry Glaze Topping

3	tablespoons apple jelly
1	teaspoon lemon juice, from concentrate
½	teaspoon cornstarch
1	teaspoon water

- In saucepan, combine apple jelly and lemon juice.
- Cook and stir until jelly melts.

 Dissolve cornstarch in 1 teaspoon of water. Add to jelly mixture.

 Cook and stir until thickened and drizzle over strawberries.

AMBROSIA TOPPING

Good on top of Cherry Cheese Pie and ice cream.

½   cup peaches or apricot preserves
¼   cup flaked coconut
2   tablespoons orange flavored liqueur
2   teaspoons cornstarch

 Combine all ingredients in small saucepan.

 Cook and stir until thickened.

 Chill thoroughly.

 To top pie, arrange fresh orange slices and drizzle with sauce.
    Yield: ½ cup

CHOCOLATE MINT DESSERT

1   cup all-purpose flour
½   cup granulated sugar
1¼   cups butter, divided
4   eggs
1½   cups Hershey's chocolate syrup
2   cups confectioner's sugar
1   tablespoon water (cont.→)

233

⅔   **teaspoon mint extract**

3   **drops green food coloring**

TOPPING

1   **cup Hershey's semisweet chocolate chips**

- Combine flour, granulated sugar, ½ cup butter, eggs and chocolate syrup.
- Beat until smooth.
- Bake in a 13x9-inch pan for 25-30 minutes at 350 degrees.
- Cool completely.
- Combine confectioner's sugar, ½ cup butter, 1 tablespoon water, mint extract and food coloring.
- Mix well.
- Spread evenly over cooked layer.
- Mix one cup chocolate chips with 6 tablespoons butter in small saucepan.
- Heat until chocolate melts.
- Pour over cooked portion.
- Chill before serving and cut into squares.

WE DETOURED OFF I-**95** TO
FLORIDA--
WORTH THE EXTRA MILES!
---NORFOLK, VIRGINIA

Index

A

Acorn Squash 110
Alice's Brownies 221
Almond and Orange Salad 79
Ambrosia Topping 233
Angel Biscuits 174
Apple Brown Betty 226
Apple Pie 192
Apple Walnut Cake 204
Apples
    51, 192, 198, 204, 225, 226, 120
Artichokes 57
Asparagus 124
Asparagus Casserole 124

B

Bacon 46, 47
Bacon Roll Ups 47
Bacon-Chestnut Appetizers 46
Baked Apples 120
Baked Beans 114
Baked Chicken 153
Baked Pineapple Casserole 122
Baked Pork Chops 143
Baked Pork Chops and Rice 142
Baked Vidalia Onions 104
Banana Nut Bread 227
Banana Pudding 228
Bananas 227, 228
Beans 113, 114, 128
Beef Stroganoff 139
Beets 119
Beverages 94, 95, 96
Bing Frozen Cherry Salad 88
Biscuits 174, 175, 176
Black-Eyed Peas 111
Blender Souffle 124
Blue Willow Squares 219
Blueberries 65, 66, 177, 224, 231, 77
Blueberry Banana Pecan Nut Cake 208
Blueberry Cobbler 224

Blueberry Dessert 231
Blueberry Muffins 177
Blueberry Salad 77
Blueberry Sauce 66
Blueberry Topping 65
Boiled Okra 108
Boiled Water 69
Bourbon Sauce 67
Bran Muffins 178
Bread Pudding 230
Breads 227
Broccoli 151
Broccoli Casserole 122
Broiled Peanut Butter Frosting 202
Brownies 222
Brunswick Stew 75
Buttermilk Biscuits 174
Buttermilk Congealed Salad 86
Buttermilk Pie 184

C

Cabbage 63, 117, 127, 84
Cabbage Casserole 127
Cabbage Relish 63
Candied Yams - Family Size 119
Candies 232
Carmelized Almonds 79
Carrot-Raisin Salad 87
Carrots 87
Casseroles
    148, 151, 156, 157, 158, 165, 166, 168
Catfish 170
Chatham Artillery Punch 96
Cheese 58, 68, 129, 151, 82, 91, 92
Cheese Cookies 48
Cheese Mold 54
Cheese Sauce 68
Cheesy Ham Potato Casserole 151
Cherries 185, 207, 88
Cherry Cheese Pie 185
Chewies 220
Chewy Oatmeal Cookies 217
Chex Party Mix 52
Chicken and Dumplings 73
Chicken and Rice 155
Chicken Casserole 157
Chicken Divine 155

236

Turkey 162
Turnip Greens 98
Twice Baked Potatoes 99

V

Vegetable Soup 74
Vegetables 74, 85
Veranda Tea Punch 94
Vidalia Onion Casserole 121
Vidalia Onions 104

W

Waldorf Salad 87
Watergate Salad 78
Watergate Salad (Green Stuff) 78
White Chocolate Macadamia Nut
Cookies 216

Y

Yams 118, 119
Yams Louie 118
Yeast Rolls 180

Z

Zucchini Squash 110

Directions to the Blue Willow Inn. Take I-20 East out of Atlanta for about 40 miles. Get off on Exit 47 (Hwy 11). Turn left and the restaurant is four miles down on the right.

IF YOU WOULD LIKE TO ORDER ADDITIONAL COPIES OF THE BLUE WILLOW INN COOKBOOK

CALL (800) 552-8813 OR (770) 464-2131
VISA, MASTERCARD OR DISCOVER ACCEPTED
OR COMPLETE THIS FORM AND MAIL

Please send me _____ copies of the Cookbook $15.95 each _____
Georgia residents add 6% sales tax   .90 each _____
Postage and handling   3.00 each _____
TOTAL ENCLOSED $_____

Name _____
Address_____
City_____State_____Zip_____
*If shipping to multiple addresses, or enclosure card needed, please attach.

Please make checks payable to:
Blue Willow Inn
294 N. Cherokee Road Ga. Hwy 11
Social Circle, GA 30279

TO REACH ST. SIMONS PRESS CALL (800) 604-0771